Angels & Franciscans

Leo Castelli/Gagosian Gallery
65 Thompson Street
Rizzoli
New York

Innovative

Architecture

from

Los Angeles

and

San Francisco

Edited by
Bill Lacy
Susan deMenil

Interview with
Frank O. Gehry

Frank O. Gehry

Craig Hodgetts & Hsin–Ming Fung

Holt Hinshaw Pfau Jones

Frank Israel

Koning Eizenberg

Lubowicki Lanier

Mark Mack

Thom Mayne, Morphosis

Eric Owen Moss

Stanley Saitowitz

Studio Works

RIZZOLI
NEW YORK

First published in the United States of America
in 1992 by Rizzoli International Publications, Inc.,
300 Park Avenue South, New York, N.Y. 10010,
in association with 65 Thompson Street
(Leo Castelli/Gagosian Gallery), New York, N.Y. 10012.

Library of Congress Cataloging-in-Publication Data
Angels & Franciscans: innovative architecture from Los Angeles and San Francisco/
Frank O. Gehry ... [et al.] ; edited by Susan deMenil and Bill Lacy.
p. cm.
"Interview with Frank O. Gehry."
Exhibition catalog.
ISBN 0-8478-1630-3
1. Architecture, Postmodern—California—Los Angeles—Exhibitions. 2. Los
Angeles (Calif.)—Buildings, structures, etc.—Exhibitions. 3. Architecture,
Postmodern—California—San Francisco—Exhibitions. 4. San Francisco (Calif.)—
Building, structures, etc.—Exhibitions. I. Gehry, Frank O., 1929– . II. deMenil,
Susan. III. Lacy, Bill. IV. Title: Angels and Franciscans.
NA735.L55A54 1992   92-19583
720'.9794'940747471—dc20   CIP

Book and jacket design by Lawrence Wolfson

This volume is the fifth in a series of Gagosian Gallery/Rizzoli, New York publications and accompanies an exhibition at Leo Castelli/Gagosian Gallery, 65
Thompson Street, New York New York, September 26 - November 6, 1992;
traveling to the Santa Monica Museum of Art, Santa Monica California,
February 4 - March 28, 1993.

Series Editor: Raymond Foye

Acknowledgments: David Morton, *senior editor;* Andrea E. Monfried, *associate
editor;* Elizabeth White, *production director;* Robert Pincus-Witten and Melissa
Lazarov, *Gagosian Gallery project coordinators.*

Special thanks to Leo Castelli

Printed and bound in Japan

Front cover:
Frank O. Gehry
Madison Square Garden, *New York, 1987.*
Model. Wood and paper, 35 x 34 x 39 in
(89 x 86 x 100 cm).

Eric Owen Moss
Nara Convention Center,
Nara, Japan, 1991. Map. Composite drawing (detail),
42 x 56 in (107 x 142 cm).

Back cover:
Holt Hinshaw Pfau Jones
'29 Chaise Longue
1990-92. Ink on mylar,
30 x 30 in (76 x 76 cm).

Contents

Foreword

Architecture proceeds from the society in which it exists; any attempt to sum up
in purely architectural terms cultures as diverse, broad, and individualistic as those
represented by Los Angeles and San Francisco can, at best, touch only on their
merely observable traits. It is said that "California is peculiarly sympathetic to the
ingenuity and daring essential to the formulation of new design concepts."[1] This
sympathy produced a Californian architecture—from the salad days of Maybeck
and the brothers Greene to the present—full of spontaneity and improvisation,
and characterized by a use of ordinary materials and homemade means of construction as well as a penchant for technologically-based, ready-made industrial materials. The result is a uniquely Californian amalgam of high and low tech.

     The idiosyncratic West Coast environment—the abundance of natural
light and deep shadows, sunbaked or saturated colors, a sense of freedom deriving
from the vast Western openness—has significantly affected its architectural purpose. The agreeable climate in California also allows for greater interplay between
interior and exterior spaces. Frequent natural catastrophes give rise to a sense of
impermanence and unease in its residents, which in turn breeds in the architecture
a wit and brashness unique to the locale. Another factor that contributes to the
novel aspects of Californian architecture is the geographical distance of the local
architects from Europe, and a proximity to the Far East. While subject to influences of both East and West, in the end they are pledged to neither.

     "Angels & Franciscans" was conceived as a show meant to explore the
generation born of the pioneering vision of Frank Gehry. Although he would
demur, and quickly rejects the idea of his having created a "school," it is undeni-
able that Gehry's work, especially, became the standard of measurement. While
none of the other ten architects in the show consider themselves to be Gehry fol-
lowers—indeed each is far too accomplished and individualistic to be thought of in
that way—they freely acknowledge that Frank Gehry created an open artistic climate of which they are all beneficiaries. They emphasize the honest expression of
materials, the idea of architecture as art, easy collaborations with other artists, a
final assault on Euclidean geometry and space, and a willingness to risk and experi-
ment—all part of the Gehry tradition. Gehry himself says, "I am interested in fin-
ishing work, but I am interested in the work's not appearing finished, with every
hair in place, every piece of furniture in its spot ready for photographs. I prefer the
sketch quality, the tentativeness, the messiness if you will, the appearance of 'in
progress' rather than the presumption of total resolution and finality. . . . I app-
roach each building as a sculptural object, a spatial container . . . with light and air,
a response to context and appropriateness of feeling and spirit. . . . In my work the
perception of the object is primary. The imagery is real and not abstract, using dis-
tortion and juxtaposition of cheap materials to create surrealistic compositions."[2]

Southern rather than Northern California is more heavily represented in this exhibition. There is, however, an easy flow of dialogue and ideas between San Francisco and Los Angeles. Many of the architects in this show are not native Californians, but represent a western migratory pattern of settlement. California is as much a destination as a specific locale. If the East coast and New York are the melting pot of European cultures created by turn-of-the-century immigrant waves, then Los Angeles and San Francisco are similar vessels for strong Pacific, Far Eastern, and Spanish influences—what one writer has referred to as "an ad hoc culture in which people and institutions make themselves up as they go along."[3]

The architects in this exhibition and catalogue were the first generation to look California culture square in the eye and say, "Well if this is what we have to work with, let's see what we can make out of it." They were the first to acknowledge that theirs was a place of cities "organized around roads and signs, not solid objects," with buildings facing an "adoring sea of parked cars";[4] in other words, a collage rather than an ordered composition. From this chaotic clutter of freeways and endless strips of meaningless buildings, they fashioned an architecture that is subject to dislocation and transformation, that is in a continuous state of dramatic tension. These architects can be thought of as doing to architecture what Picasso and Braque did to conventional painting when Cubism challenged long-honored traditions of space, movement, and time. With this challenge, these architects have fashioned a new spatial aesthetic and are evolving a new perspective with which to view architectural design.

Bill Lacy and Susan deMenil

Notes

1. Thomas Leavitt, Introduction to *California design/eight* (Pasadena: Pasadena Art
    Museum, 1962), 7.
2. Muriel Emanuel, ed., *Contemporary Architects* (New York: St. Martins Press,
    1980), 279.
3. Leon Whiteson, "Young Architects in Los Angeles: The Social, Political and Cultural
    Context," in *Experimental Architecture in Los Angeles* (New York:
    Rizzoli, 1991), 87.
4. Aaron Betsky, "Building (in) the Brave New World," in *Experimental Architecture in
    Los Angeles* (New York: Rizzoli, 1991), 44.

Interview

*As an architect, I believe that we have all now entered an era in
which the city of the future is not going to be built by a Frank Lloyd
Wright, or a Le Corbusier. Those visions are gone. The work that
was built was idiosyncratic and didn't solve the social problems. I
think the only direction for architecture to go in today's world is
toward greater connection with media and computers and art. We
architects have to accept the collaborative stance.* F.G.

Bill Lacy: I want to talk about influences. Had you stayed in Toronto instead of
relocating to the West coast, would your architecture have been different?

**Frank Gehry: I don't think I would even be an architect.
I didn't know I wanted to be an architect, but there was one
sign of it: When I was sixteen I used to go to the University
of Toronto—they had a lecture series. None of my friends
would go with me; it was something I had to do by myself.
Every Friday night I would go to the University of Toronto
to hear these lectures. When I was sixteen—1946 or so—
I remember a gentleman coming out on the stage with a plywood chair, and showing this chair. He was from Finland.
He showed some buildings, but I wasn't really interested in
buildings. I was interested in that goddam chair. The image
of that chair was in my head. I didn't remember this architect's name, but years later, when I was in Finland, I visited
Alvar Aalto, and I said, "Were you in Toronto in 1946?"
And sure enough he said yes. I carried that image for years.
I still do, I still remember that night, the man with the
chair. I wasn't even interested in architecture. I wanted to
be a chemical engineer. I was doing chemistry things in my
house and lab.**

BL: So where did you study architecture?

**FG: I didn't study architecture until I came out to L.A. I left
Toronto at seventeen, and the following year moved to Los
Angeles, did the truck driver thing, went to high school. Oh
God, I had a hard time figuring out what I wanted to be
when I grew up. See, the role model in our family was a
chemical engineer. But in Toronto in high school, the last
year I was there, in one of those vocational guidance classes, the General Electric chemical engineering representative
came to the school and spoke. I went up after the lecture
and talked to him. He invited me out to the lab, and he took**

the time to spend the whole day with me, and at the end of the day he said, "I don't think this is for you. I've been watching you. You get excited about the adventure but you don't get excited about what we have to do to get there." He really threw me for a loop, but he sort of got me. So when I arrived in Los Angeles I didn't know what the hell I was going to do. I drove a truck, and I took art classes. I took one drawing class in architecture, because—I've told this story before: when I was a kid my grandmother used to play with me on the floor in Toronto with blocks and make cities. It's a great story because it shows you that adults playing creatively with kids is a really crucial thing. It was because of this that I took a drawing class in architecture. And I failed it. The guy said, "You can't draw worth shit." And that pissed me off, so I went back and did it again and I got an A. But I was desperate to get an A in something. Emotionally, you know. The family was having a hard time. . . .

BL: Then you went to work for Victor Gruen Associates after you graduated?

FG: Well, I worked as a truck driver for three or four years, and I took Fine Arts drawing classes at U.S.C. Then I took a night class in architecture, and I did so well they skipped me ahead to the second year. It was a major victory. But then my teacher called me in and said, "You ain't gonna make it as an architect." This guy was head architect of the Los Angeles International airport—LAX. They didn't like the way I drew. It wasn't precise enough, it was too wiggly. No, I hadn't started the wiggly stuff, it was kind of impressionistic. They didn't like it; they thought it was unprofessional. That got me madder than hell, and it scared me, too. By then, though, I had it in my gut. The passion was starting to build and I knew I wanted to do this. Then I met some teachers who started to give me positive feedback. Not for my architecture as much as for my thinking. You know, I was a Jewish liberal so I hung out with the political crowd—this was during the McCarthy era. I was into politics heavy. We were dealing with social structures in cities: political science. I attracted attention because I was one of the few people in the whole school who even thought

about such things, besides a few of the teachers. Most of the
kids didn't want to hear about that.

BL: Then what did you do?

FG: I made a great effort to learn how to draw.

BL: When did you graduate?

FG: 1954.

BL: And how long was it before you set up your own practice?

FG: 1962.

BL: Eight years, kicking around. . .

FG: I went in the army for two years—Fort Benning,
Georgia. I was an enlisted man, not an officer.

BL: How come they didn't put you in the Corps of Engineers?

FG: Well, they tried. The Corps of Engineers was getting
ready to go out on maneuvers in the field. I have a bad leg,
the knee joint. I had gone through basic training as a cler-
ical typist. So when the Corps of Engineers called me in,
supposedly as the company clerk, after about thirty minutes
into things they knew they had a ringer! They said, "If you
can't do this, what can you do?" I said, "Well I can draw."
They said, "Fine, make some signs for the latrine: Don't
throw paper in the latrine." So I did six or seven signs. I
really went all out. And the guy looked at those signs and
said, "What have we got here. " Later at the Officers Club
he happened to be bragging to somebody about this crazy
guy he'd got and didn't know what to do with. And they
said, "Well, we're getting ready to go on maneuvers, and
this General needs charts made—can this guy get a top security clearance?" Now, I was in all those left-wing organiza-
tions! So they called me in and said, "Private Gehry, we
have a new job for you. We're gonna send you over to headquarters to work for the General, and you've got to get top
security clearance—is there anything we should know
about?" I said, "No, I don't think so" (laughing). I used to
march with Linus Pauling. Anyway, they believed me and
the General gave me a battlefield security clearance. See,
they loved these drawings I made! Next I had a room in a
warehouse where I was all alone, and they would bring in
these charts of how the tanks would move and how the air-

craft were going to fit. It was some new maneuver they were going to try out, with small intense groups that would charge behind the lines; it was a system where they would create a micro-army. So I made these charts. It got pretty busy so they got another guy, and he worked for me. I had this workshop, and we made some of the most elegant signs and charts. The General loved them because he would go before these committees and the charts were legible and looked good, and the colors were nice. I had a great time. I would embellish the insignia—my medieval instincts came out. I actually got into calligraphy. . . . But my leg used to hurt me because of all the running I did in basic. I used to go to the infirmary to get heat treatments on my leg, and I got to know the doctor, who was from Montgomery, Alabama. When he heard I was an architect, he would wait for me to come in, and for an hour he would have me design a clinic for him, to build when he got out of the army.

BL: Your first commission!

FG: I'll tell you what happened because of this doctor—it was amazing. My whole life is like this. I think there must be methods to this madness, somewhere in my head. The General who was in charge of maneuvers also went to this doctor, and they were talking about me, I guess, and the doctor said, "You better not take Gehry out into the field because of his bum leg." The General called me a month before they were leaving, and he said, "I've gotten a call from Atlanta, from Fort MacPherson, and they're looking for somebody who can draw, I think you fit this bill. I'm recommending you for transfer to Fort MacPherson." So, bon voyage! We had a great time. I even designed field latrines, which were funny as hell. They looked like Frank Lloyd Wright. I also designed dayrooms and service clubs. The first ones looked very Frank Lloyd Wright. I was very much into him at the time.

BL: You were in the army from 1954 until when?

FG: 1956. Then I went to Harvard graduate school from '56 to '57. I had worked for Gruen in the summer of '53, and then in '54 after graduation, until I got drafted.

BL: When you came out of Harvard there was a period from '57 to '62, before you started your own practice.

FG: Yes, and I went to work for Bill Pereira.

BL: So from Toronto all the way to Los Angeles was quite a distance. I gave a lecture in Europe—it must have been the early 1970s—and I showed your work, and nobody had ever heard of you anywhere. I remember you kept saying, "I want to get back East, everythings's happening out there." But then you kept staying on in L.A. And pretty soon it kind of started coming to you, the Far Eastern influence, which was so important for Frank Lloyd Wright. Was it your being isolated out there, and getting in with the artists' group rather than the architects' group, that influenced you; was it climate, was it social?

FG: A little bit of everything. When I got out of school I had a lot of Japanese classical influences—Hiroshigi fish drawings and Tatami mats. . . . There was Gordon Drake, Wayne Williams, Bill Rudolph, and Quincy Jones—all influenced by Japanese design. Then Harwell Harris was doing work out here, and that was beautiful stuff, such as the Chrysanthemum Lane house. All of that, in Southern California, did fit into my Japanophile memory systems, and with it came a sense of order that was different from Western classicism. I was really bitten by it; in fact, my friends used to say I was bitten by the Japanese beetle. And I think that when you see what happened to music and literature—when the Europeans moved out here—they also got it. The most recent example of somebody who turned East when he got here was David Hockney. But this happened to Thomas Mann, it happened to Arnold Schoenberg, it happened to Igor Stravinsky and many more. But a lot of my generation was influenced by the East because they were in the army; they'd just got back from Japan, and they'd seen it all.

BL: Does the early California architecture mean anything to you?

FG: The problem with California Spanish colonial architecture in my perception is that it was being ripped off left and right by the developers, trivialized. By the time I got here the building boom was on. The Spanish colonialism was too soft, although I did some buildings like that—Kay Jewelers Offices and Warehouse (1963). Looks like a marriage between Spanish colonial and Japan.

BL: Philip Johnson is an influence you've cited several times, not so much on your work but on your ability to survive and practice. You've said that he created the climate in which it was easier for you and a lot of other people to practice.

FG: I think that's true. And he's a role model as well. Whatever you think of Philip's work, his generosity to younger people is tremendous.

BL: Which brings me to the fact that you are not entirely comfortable when people say that you have a big influence on the next generation of California architects. There's obviously something that holds all of you together in some way, or that makes whatever you do out there have certain similarities—whether it's from seeing each other's work, or whether it's from being that close to the Pacific Ocean, or standing out in the sun too long, or something. . . .

FG: Well I've figured it out for myself anyway, and this may or may not be true, but I was recently on a jury for the Academy, and we had ten young architects including Eric Owen Moss and many others. (This was in New York.) And it became obvious to me that the real influence, aesthetically, is not Frank Gehry, but Carlo Scarpa, and Thom Mayne and Morphosis, because they have started an architecture of detail. All the work submitted showed pictures of stairways. The first picture in everybody's proposal was of a stairway with a weird handrail, and then a light fixture at the end of a hall. It was fragments of buildings. Now maybe I'm the one who started looking at fragments—the fracturing of buildings—I don't know. I don't think so—I think it was in the air—but I see Scarpa in that, and it's not at all what I'm interested in. If you look at Thom Mayne, and Eric Moss, and recently Frank Israel—except for their occasional use of galvanized steel or something like that—I think their detailing and attitude is quite different from my own.

I'm not interested in all that detailing. People like it, but with me it's more of a Jewish lib thing—it's about not flaunting your riches. All that fussy detail, it's pretentious, in a way. I don't mean to indict all of them, because I really like them, but that's where I go off the other side. I'm making the case that they aren't really influenced by me—I may have been what broke the line of the enemy.

BL: Right, I think you did for them what Johnson did for you. I think you gave them a spirit, and you gave them a license to do what they wanted to do.

> FG: Yeah, and I guess by example it showed them that you could do little buildings, and you could get satisfaction from them.

BL: That's Japanese too.

> FG: In the early days when I came up and started practicing, the artists showed an interest in my work. I would find artists whom I knew by name but had never met climbing around in my construction sites—like Ed Moses, Ron Davis, Billy Al Bengston. So slowly I was pulled into the art scene, more by Ed Moses than by anyone. I got a lot of positive support from the artists, which I wasn't getting from the architects. The architects thought I was weird.

BL: Do you think that your work now is becoming too risky for clients on one hand, and too predictable on the other?

> FG: You mean "predictable" in that they know I'm gonna do something different?

BL: That some of them are afraid of you because they can sense what you're gonna do: "Oh no I don't wanna do that because that's just gonna be another Gehry building."

> FG: Well, that last part I can't relate to. I see all my work as one thing. I see it as all one kind of language, like Mies van der Rohe, believe it or not. But I push forward on imagery. I'm interested in the movement of buildings, the sense of movement. I was taken with the Shiva dancing figures, the frozen motion—a feeling that you could approach sculpture—that has always interested me, that fluidity. And by accident, really, I started playing with the fish horn and discovered the feeling and the movement, and I was able to build some of those double-curved structures quite easily and not terribly expensively. It sort of demystified the structures for me and led me down that path. So it's a continuum.

BL: I picked up a book on Frederick Keistler the other day and I thought about you because of some of the spaces inside. Did the Endless House or anything by Keistler ever mean anything to you?

> FG: Yes, I looked at all that.

BL: I was just curious because Keistler tried to do curves and get out of the recti-linear box and never quite made it. Most people give up when they get to curved surfaces.

FG: Erich Mendelsohn did it.

BL: You once said that every building you did has its own discipline. I mean, you bring to it the same kind of discipline that Mies brought to a building, but you still have to solve the problem of circulation and flow and environment.

FG: See, I can never understand why somebody's afraid of what I do, because once a client goes through the process with me they really are quite comfortable—because I am able to explain what I'm trying to do in simple English words to such a great degree that they understand in advance where I'm going. I give them the story quite directly—and they can influence it.

A very interesting thing happened with David Steadman—I finished the design and he loved it. Then as I was working on trying to solve window details in this tough building that shouldn't have windows—that's the difference between sculpture and architecture, the windows—and I was struggling with these windows and started to fudge it by mak-ing overhangs. I sent him a model with that, and he called me one day and said, "I have to come and see you face to face—you've taken a direction with the building that is absolutely the opposite of what you and I agreed on, and I don't like it, nobody here likes it, and we have a crisis." I looked at both models and the difference were these eye-brows I was putting in to fudge the window thing. He flew all the way out to Los Angeles on a Saturday morning to see me and to look me in the eye and tell me that I was ruining the building as far as they were concerned, and that he would not approve the new design. The new design represented a two percent change from the other one, except for these eyebrows. I kept looking at him and wondering, "What the hell's he talking about?" We went round and round for about three hours and finally I said: "David, you have been so involved in the process with me from the beginning that you're kinda like my conscience here, and I'm gonna trust your judgement and rethink this thing." Which I did—thank

God—and we solved the problem properly. So there is an involvement with the client that can be better and healthier than working in isolation or with fixed ideas. It's not as scary once you get into it.

BL: Does the individual house now come off as kind of a note in a larger symphony that you're doing?

FG: Well, we're working in Frankfurt on such a project—with social housing. We're doing master planning and layouts of streets and greenbelts. Very low-budget buildings. There are no individual houses in these things, but I like doing these housing blocks. If the plan goes ahead, I would try to bring in other people. I don't try to do it all myself now. I wouldn't suggest that I have a vision. The only vision I have is that it's got to be a collaborative vision. For instance, David Childs and I are now trying to work on Madison Square Garden in New York, and there are many collaborators. It's an eclectic, changeable, movable project. And it's different from the model of Prince Charles.

Penn Station/Madison Square Garden Redevelopment

This competition project, won in collaboration with Skidmore, Owings & Merrill, was planned as a renovation of the Madison Square Garden site located above Pennsylvania Station in midtown Manhattan. The development was to include approximately 4.5 million square feet of new construction over the train station, in addition to planned improvements of the railway and pedestrian areas.

The major development consists of four elements: a 70-story north office tower designed by SOM; a 61-story south office tower of approximately 1.7 million square feet designed by Frank O. Gehry & Associates; a 24-story east office tower; and a canopy joining the three towers near the base. The latter two elements were designed as a collaboration between the two firms. Essentially, the canopy forms a covered grand-hall entrance to Penn Station, while the three towers rise from a single 90-foot-high plinth, which houses high-quality retail space as well as the office lobbies.

FOG/A's south tower design consists of a 61-story rectilinear armature flanked by a 57-story knife-edged wedge and a 55-story fish form, with a cubic penthouse structure on top. The curvilinear office tower is sheathed in sandblasted stainless steel panels punctured with clear glass windows. At present, the project has been delayed at least ten years due to market conditions.

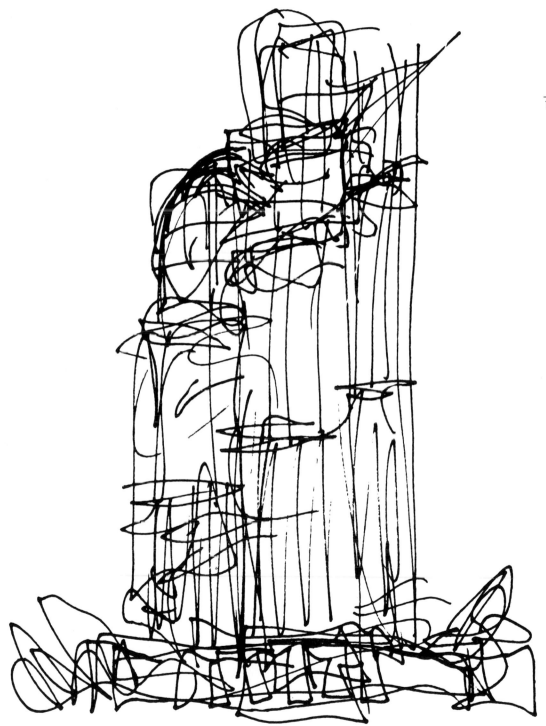

Madison Square Garden, *1987.*
Model. Wood and paper,
35 x 34 x 39 in
(89 x 86 x 100 cm).

F
R
A
N
K

O

G
E
H
R
Y

Madison Square Garden, *1987.*
Model. Wood and paper,
35 x 34 x 39 in
(89 x 86 x 100 cm).

F
R
A
N
K

O

G
E
H
R
Y

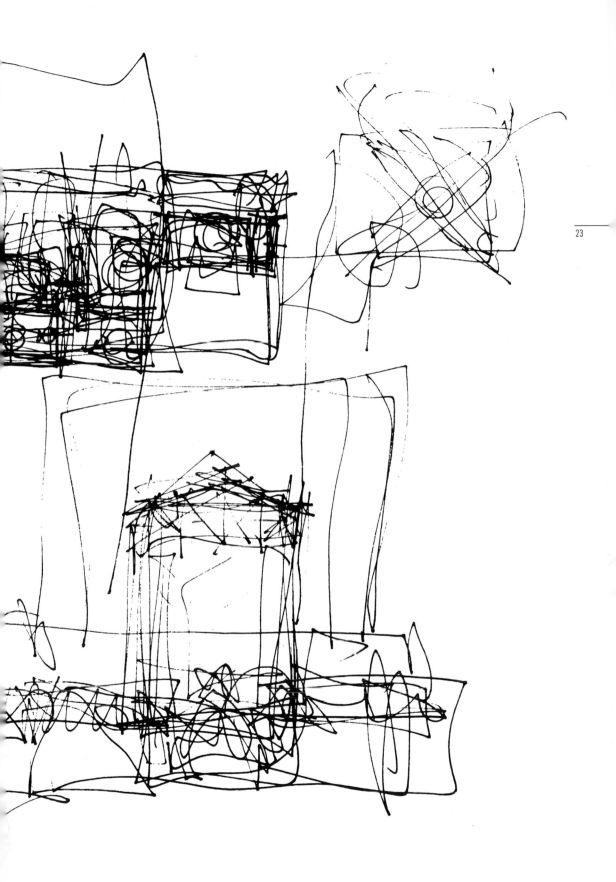

Madison Square Garden, *1987.*
Ink on paper, 9 x 12 in
(23 x 30 cm).

Madison Square Garden, *1987.*
Model. Wood,
13 x 8 x 12 in
(33 x 20 x 30 cm).

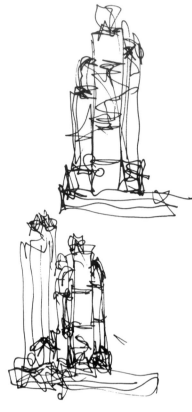

Visions of San Francisco
Studies for Skinner's Room

CRAIG HODGETTS & HSIN-MING FUNG

Architecture as seen by various writers through time has consistently inspired me by identifying the role that architecture can play in expanding and amplifying the human condition. Victor Hugo, Italo Calvino, Raymond Chandler, E.B. White, and other writers underscore the role that environment plays in the developing drama of life.

When I first read the work of William Gibson, it struck me that he had single-handedly generated the next strata. There is a fecund, fearsomely tangible physical presence to the streets he envisions that propels the story and involves the characters in far more than the cybernetic world that he is popularly identified with. Gibson's eye is that of a pack rat roaming through junkyards and back alleys picking up the miscellany. When Gibson sits down at the typewriter with his grab bag of appliances, rusting structures, billboards, and abandoned monuments, he assembles a new order of utility as well as an uncanny sort of conceptual beauty.

One story in particular inspired these drawings. It is called "Skinner's Room," and it suggests that the hulk of the San Francisco Bay Bridge, like the hulk of other similar structures, may someday provide the locus for a new community which has evolved in a techno-organic fashion. Gibson's vision of San Francisco suggests a time to come when handsome monuments and good housekeeping are not enough, a time when careless consumption and predatory development have all but exhausted the natural resources and human spirit which were the foundation of its charm.

Another reality flickers through the window of Skinner's Room. It is the reality of soft tech, dead tech, no tech. It is a plastic-cybernetic bio-haven for the living. It is memories of printouts, and stacks and stacks of unorganized data. It is leather and beer cans and knives and inexplicable tenderness. It is life between the layers of history now, then, or sometime.

These drawings are my attempt to give form to the Gibson vision.

Preceding page
Visions of San Francisco:
Skinner's Room, "A Magnet for
the Restless," *1992.*
*Charcoal and pastel on canary
paper,*
34 x 18 in (86 x 46 cm).

Visions of San Francisco: Skinner's Room, "Sunflower Corporation," *1990–92. Model. Mixed media, 144 x 33 x 13 1/2 in (366 x 84 x 34 cm).*

Visions of San Francisco:
Skinner's Room, *1990.*
Felt-tip pen on bond paper,
11 x 8 1/2 in (28 x 22 cm).

C
R
A
I
G

H
O
D
G
E
T
T
S

&

H
S
I
N
-
M
I
N
G

F
U
N
G

Visions of San Francisco:
Skinner's Room, *1990.*
Felt-tip pen on bond paper,
17 x 11 in (43 x 28 cm).

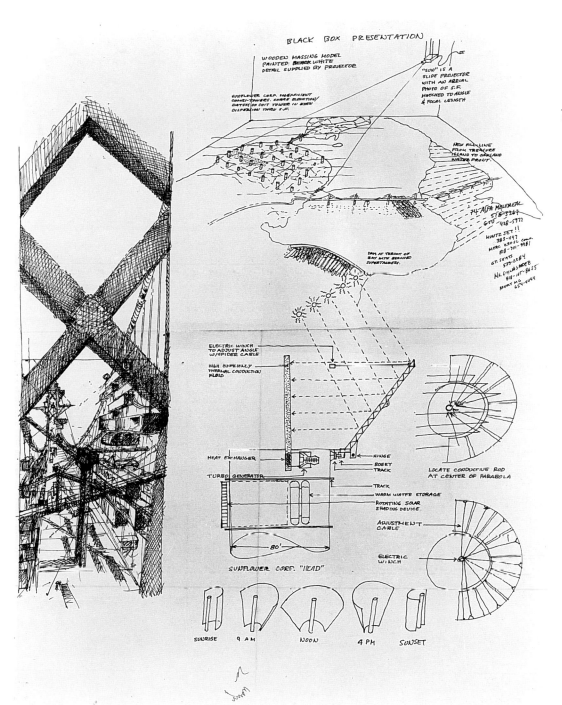

Visions of San Francisco:
Skinner's Room, "Intricate
Barrios," *1992.*
*Charcoal and pastel on canary
paper,*
9 1/4 x 16 1/4 in (24 x 41cm).

Visions of San Francisco:
Skinner's Room, "An Accretion
of Dreams," *1992.*
*Charcoal and pastel on canary
paper,*
9 x 16 in (23 x 41 cm).

Visions of San Francisco:
Skinner's Room, "Makeshift
Ligatures," *1992.*
Charcoal and pastel on canary paper,
31 x 14 in (79 x 36 cm).

"Soup's Up—"

There is one strategy of interventive re-use which, though critical, carries none of the negative sense that we expect from critique: the adaptive re-use strategy called "souping-up," used primarily by young automotive enthusiasts to create Hot Rods.

The host for the souping-up intervention is not chosen casually. Not just any old jalopy will do; the chosen jalopy is rescued from the scrapyard and lovingly restored; as much effort is spent rendering the body immaculate as in upgrading the power plant. In this way, many otherwise forgotten vehicles have achieved a classic status. It is through their souped-up versions, blessed by this process of sanctification-by-intervention, that we have come to revere the '56 Chevy, the Woody, the '34 Ford, the Datsun 510, or '69 Mustang.

The critique embodied in souping-up follows the logic of supplementation: the intervention acts as "something which completes or makes an addition (Webster)." The supplement is "an inessential extra, added to something complete in itself, but [it] is added in order to complete, to compensate for a lack in what was supposed to be complete in itself (Culler 103)." In the case of the jalopy it is clear that the original vehicle—even if run-down—remains sufficient to the task of transportation and thus could be considered complete. Yet, it is just as clear that, in regarding these vehicles from the distance of time and increased expectation—that is, from the perspective of the enthusiast—they do seem to suffer a certain dorkiness.

These are everyman's vehicles—family cars and working vehicles—with expectations encouraged by lowest common denominator marketing and realized through the universalization of mass production. The assembly line promise of two-cars-in-every-garage intends to lead to the freedom of wide open spaces. This is essentially meaningless if all these spaces, cars, and garages are the same. But it is precisely this aspect which is addressed by the souping process: making the hot rod a statement of the importance of the individual in contrast to the anonymous conformity of the assembly line. The statement made by the souped-up vehicle is all about the vehicle's power and speed, but the critique is about empowering the individual, opening up these spaces to the freedom they hide.

When applied to architecture, supplement usually means ornamentation; the essence which casts ornament as supplemental is not uniqueness (since this is unavoidable) but apparent (purpose). The modern movement attempted to strip away the supplementary decoration that was suffocating architecture, to prove that this decoration did not redress an essential lack, but in fact, if anything, the essence was apparently lacking because of the surplus of this supplement. The common essentiality of purpose, or function, was recovered then by paring the object down to the purest statement of that purpose of function.

The "Chaise Longue, a *relage continu*" by Le Corbusier and Charlotte Perriand, first shown to the public at the Salon d'Automne of 1929, was modelled on a bentwood chaise longue already produced for years by Thonet. This upgraded "machine for rest" quickly became an icon of modern functional furniture design. The grace, abstraction, and purity of its lines paid homage to the chief formgivers of the age: the steamship, the airplane, and the humble objets d'universal of mass production. It was designed for everyman as a pure statement of rest, assembled with components from the steamship and airplane, into an "objet type" that showed how this engineers' aesthetic could be applied to the objects of the everyday environment.

The engineers' aesthetic holds the value of efficiency uppermost— finding the highest value in the transparency of an object to its function. The pre-conventional significance made apparent in this transparency challenged the eclecticism of the nineteenth century as well as the traditional decorative encrustation smothering the object. Considered in contrast as a naked embodiment of function alone, the object is clearly liberated.

This sort of transparency is, however, contrary to an understanding of architecture as an expressive medium. When function is interpreted primarily in terms of a satisfaction of physical needs, this message of liberation delivered by the object as a direct embodiment of function is condemned to trivial statements of shelter and hygiene. In such a case, architecture's traditional responsibility for a lofty expression of the ideals and aspirations of the age is forsaken for a more prosaic representation of its standards of comfort and sanitation. The transparent embodiment of function which shapes airplanes or steamships and makes mass production profitable (through a universalization of technique) is at odds with an expression that, as a significant opacity, favors the signifier over the signified.

The adoption of the machine as a visual referent by the modern movement was not in itself inappropriate—the contrast between the machines for living and the more conservative cultural artifacts of the time expressed a spirit of newness that, during the revolution, was indeed lofty. But the movement's narrow interpretation of this referent, conditioned by reaction to the excesses of the nineteenth century, could remain vital only as long as that contrast between old and new remained. This contrast was clearly stated by the emerging technology, but just as clearly some instances of

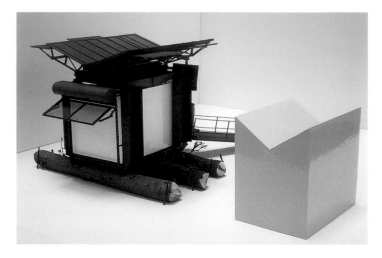

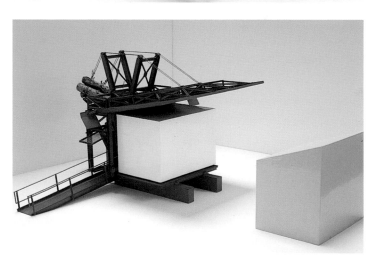

Either/Origins:
Primitive Hut, *1987.*
Model. Mixed media,
12 x 12 x 24 in
(30 x 30 x 61 cm).

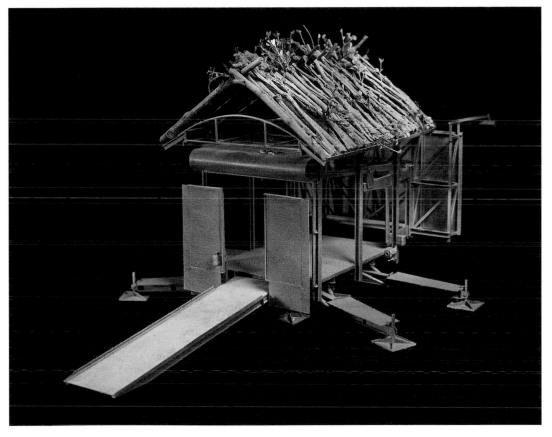

this technology were more exemplary than others. Those machines, like airplanes and grain silos, which for functional or economic reasons resisted supplementary ornamentation, were raised up as the new standard, while those that welcomed or tolerated such elaboration were overlooked. The former's abstraction and streamlined efficiency became architecture's goal, while the visual interest and elaboration offered by otherwise equally sophisticated technology was regarded with suspicion. This was an ominous distinction to make, and the post-modern critique records the legacy of sterile work that resulted.

Of course, only in retrospect can we see that it might have been the result of a wrong turn. At the time, there was no apparent forking of the path, no sense of misgiving at opportunities missed or cries of dismay by babies being tossed out with the bath water. How could this have happened? We postulate: Alien Intervention.

We figure that sometime during the summer of 1916, before that fateful fork had been reached, Le Corbusier was visited by aliens. The aliens were frightened by mankind's aggressive technological advance. Understanding that revolution was the means by which humans announced their yearning, but that architecture was the means by which they established it, the aliens contacted the future Le Corbusier. Aliens can be persuasive; they steered Le Corbusier in a direction that they knew would ultimately stifle future development.

The aliens knew that while human technology was developing at an impressive pace, human emotional maturity with respect to this development lagged far behind. They knew the only real impediment they could place in the human's path was misunderstanding. The aliens were smart: knowing that humanity was inextricably tied to its technology, they did not attempt to encourage a rejection of technology. They knew that they could ensure stagnation only by encouraging conditions that would prevent humans from embracing and emotionally integrating this technology. So, they had lunch with Le Corbusier. They told him to forget about L'Eplattenier and all that nature stuff. They talked about the importance of novelty over tradition and how far one could go with a statement that would contrast the two. They extolled the wonders of flight and the magic encapsulated in even the most reductive objet types of industry and commerce—like the Thonet Longue— they filled his vision with ideal images of pure, simple volumes at magnificent play in light, and then blinded one of his eyes to make certain that space would become abstract.

So the Thonet Longue became the Chaise Longue, a "relage continu" or a continuous adjustment; the Parthenon was purified into the Villa

'29 Chaise Longue, *1990–92.*
Plan. Ink on mylar,
30 x 30 in (76 x 76 cm).

Savoye; likewise the Model T became the '92 Taurus. These were not just any old jalopies; they certainly did not become hot rods.

By convincing Le Corbusier to prefer the abstract side of the machine, the aliens kept the machine at a distance and prevented its assimilation. By putting it on a pedestal, they ensured its ultimate alienation. The aliens feared that if humans accepted the machine as a normal extension and glorification of their humanity, then the alienation they carefully cultivated would be transformed into celebratory expressions of engagement in the world. The universe would then be open to humankind and no safe place for aliens.

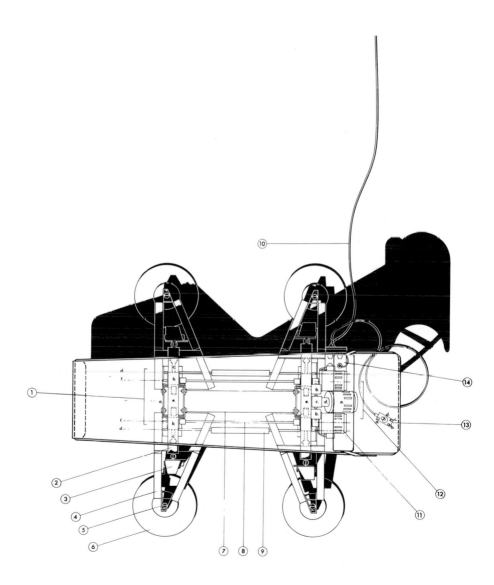

Lifeguard Tower, *1989.*
Model. Mixed media,
30 x 30 x 45 in
(76 x 76 x 114 cm).

'29 Chaise Longue, *1992.*
Mixed media on board,
two panels, each 30 x 30 in
(76 x 76 cm).

'29 Chaise Longue, *1990–92.*
Steel, chrome, plastic, elastic,
and pony hide,
30 x 77 x 23 in
(76 x 195 x 58 cm).

Molten Metal Shelter

F
R
A
N
K

I
S
R
A
E
L

Two houses cast in molten aluminum: boats at the edge of a city. Metal helmets reflect light from canal and ocean. Molded forms folded like origami give shelter and identity. Each celebrates its proximity to the sea like sails holding wind rising to the occasion.

Molten metal symbolizes the process from which forms evolve. Formal armature grows from program and site. Hague House is a home on many levels. Different spaces are topped by a folded hat. Baldwin House is two homes in one: a duplex in California terms. Here, the roof unifies and characterizes the whole. Hague House sits on a square. The square becomes a cube from which solids and voids are carved. Azure-glazed masonry walls, roofed with violet titanium shingles, are molded in silver gray. Baldwin House, in Venice Beach, is an alley house elongated like a water wave cutting a concrete block. It is gray and silver gray.

Etchings in metal—titanium sketches—set into molded glass represent these maquettes. They also draw a Hollywood home: an homage to Chaplin's *Limelight*, a linear reflection in metal of that place very near where he filmed. Thinly drawn lines, etched in azure tones, cold memories of things past and present.

Metal molded and scratched, aluminum objects and titanium sheets describe an architecture of volume and plane. A spiritual abstraction of form and material, site and program, is what this work is about. Thinly drawn, the heat of transfer from idea to reality is solidified and given place.

Locus est humane.

Hague House, *The Hague,
The Netherlands, 1991.
Ink on paper,
8 1/2 x 11in (21 x 28 cm).*

Hague House, *Northwest
Elevation, 1991.
Ink on mylar,
18 x 20 in
(46 x 51 cm).*

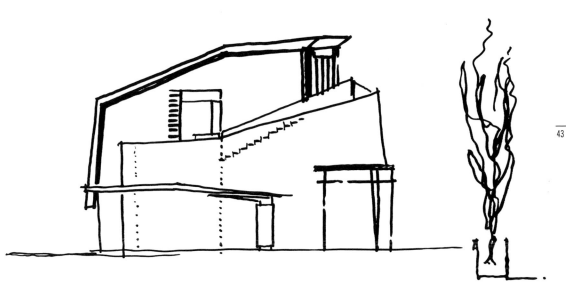

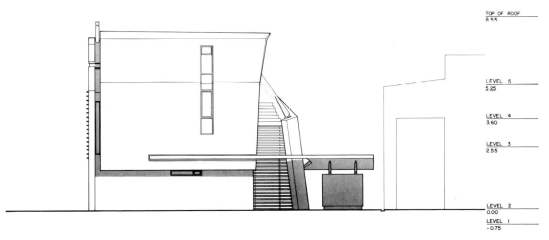

TOP OF ROOF
8.55

LEVEL 5
5.25

LEVEL 4
3.60

LEVEL 3
2.55

LEVEL 2
0.00

LEVEL 1
- 0.75

N·W ELEVATION

Hague House, *1992.*
Model. Bass wood,
6 3/4 x 6 1/8 x 6 5/8 in
(17 x 16 x 17 cm).

F
R
A
N
K

I
S
R
A
E
L

Hague House, *1992.*
Etching on titanium,
32 x 14 in (81 x 36 cm).

Baldwin House, *Level 3, Venice Beach, California, 1991.*
Ink on mylar,
18 x 20 in
(46 x 51 cm).

Baldwin House, *1991.*
Ink on paper,
8 1/2 x 11 in
(21 x 28 cm).

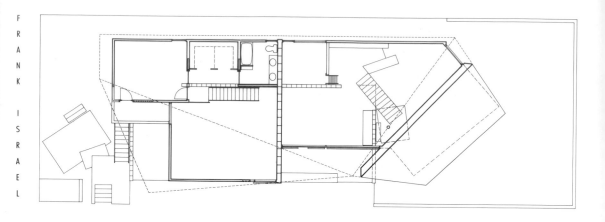

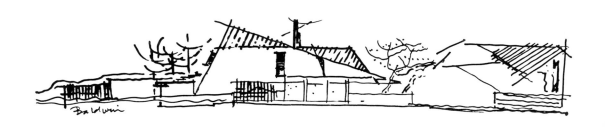

Baldwin House, *1992.*
Model. Bass wood,
7 1/2 x 16 1/2 x 4 1/2 in
(19 x 42 x 11 cm).

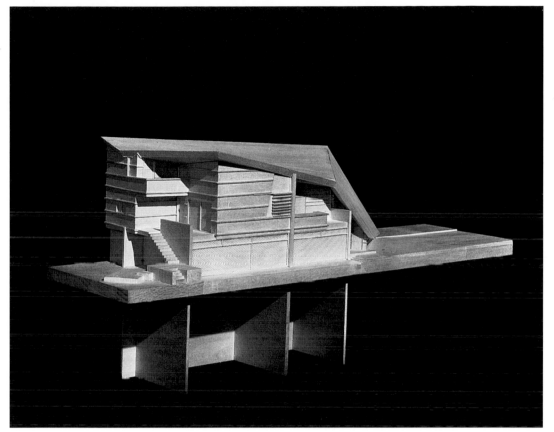

Baldwin House, *Venice Beach,*
California, 1992.
Etching on titanium,
7 1/2 x 7 1/2 in (19 x 19 cm).

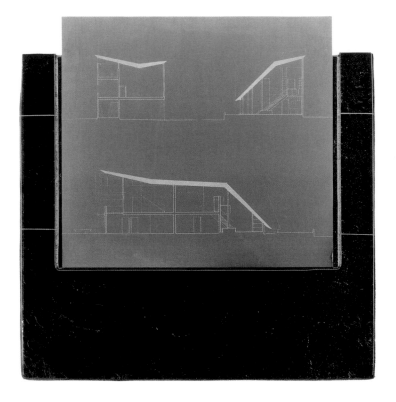

Limelight Productions,
Hollywood, California, 1992.
Etching on titanium,
12 x 4 1/2 in (30 x 11 cm).

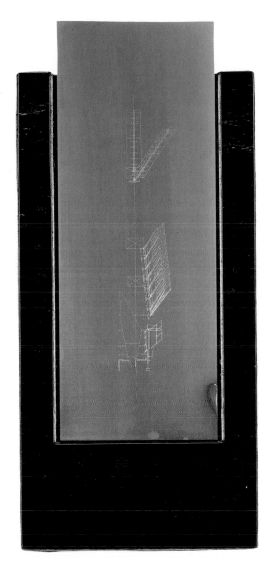

Electric ArtBlock Artist's Housing

Our drawings reflect an ambivalence about the idea of architectural drawing as art. In an era when obscurantism dominates the presentation of architecture, in an overload of overlaid images, often more complicated than the actual building, we present an abstract, reductive image of our work. The drawing works as a starting point to understand the built work, not as a theoretical explanation of it.

We see drawing in architecture as a tool, not an end in itself. We draw to design, to test approaches, and to generate ideas. Our presentation drawings are very similar to our sketches, only more carefully constructed. They too are a tool, to help our clients, and the public, better understand the basic design intentions of our buildings. They have a quality often seen as the "first sketch"—the proverbial party drawing on a napkin—only they are a result of the design process. They are, in fact, done very quickly, after careful composition. Their abstraction focuses on the fundamental compositional strategies that are a signature of our work.

Architecture, for us, is an opportunity to reassess simple pleasures—light, air, view, color, and natural beauty. We strive for accessibility to design and our drawings reflect this.

The Electric ArtBlock is a twenty-unit artist's loft building, on a 50-by 330-foot abandoned streetcar easement in Venice, California. The 330-foot frontage faces a mix of small apartment buildings across Electric Avenue and backs onto a low-scale commercial strip.

Five simple stucco blocks are strung along the streets by angled walls of sheet metal and glass, recalling the movement of the old streetcar.

Behind a formal simplicity lies a complex variety of units. The complexity—resulting from strict zoning regulations, maximum floor areas and ceiling heights, and a compact parking plan—is subtly expressed within the composition of the stucco blocks and the sheet metal ends. The south elevation is unified to provide outdoor spaces and a more rhythmic facade.

This project is constructed on commercially zoned land and utilizes the city's district-specific zoning.

This project achieves the following:

1. Since the project is intended as work-live spaces, it reaches the ultimate job-housing balance, thereby reducing traffic generation;

2. It uses commercially zoned land for residential use;

3. It establishes a housing prototype, namely the new artist-in-residence, multifamily housing type.

Preceding page
Electric Art Block, *Venice, California,*
1989.
Model. Chipboard, paint, metal, and
photograph,
6 x 28 x 4 1/2 in (15 x 71 x 11 cm).

K
O
N
I
N
G

E
I
Z
E
N
B
E
R
G

Electric ArtBlock, *1989.*
Zerograph with pantone paper,
6 x 28 in (15 x 71 cm).

Electric ArtBlock, *1989.*
Model. Chipboard, paint, metal,
and photograph,
6 x 28 x 4 1/2 in (15 x 71 x 11 cm).

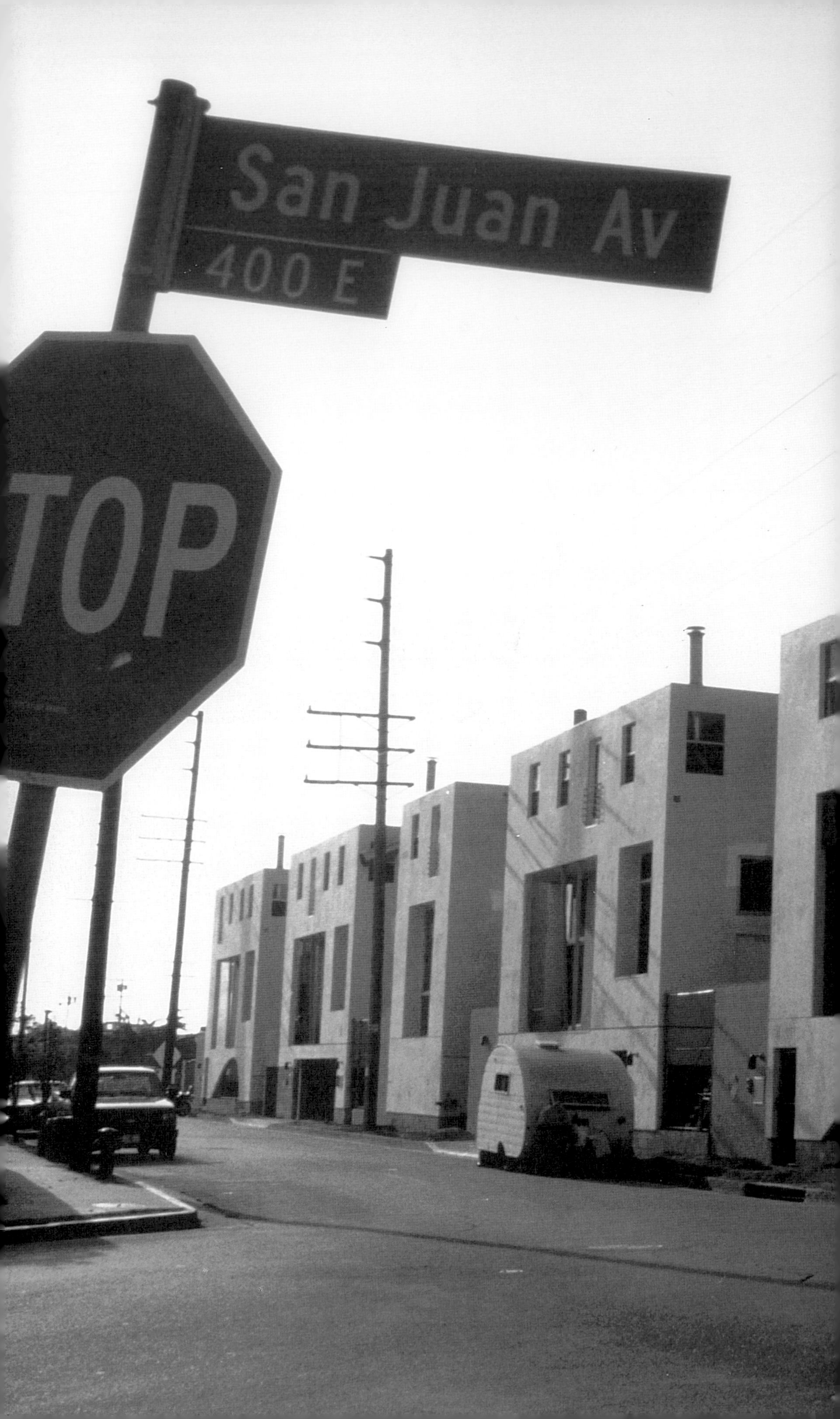
San Juan Av
400 E
TOP

Preceding pages
Electric Art Block, *1990.*
Photograph.

Electric Art Block, *1989.*
Zerograph with pantone paper,
4 x 5 1/2 in (14 x 10 cm).

Electric Art Block, *1989.*
Zerograph with pantone paper,
4 x 5 1/2 in (14 x 10 cm).

Electric Art Block, *1990.*
Photograph.

K
O
N
I
N
G

E
I
Z
E
N
B
E
R
G

O'Neill Guesthouse

L
U
B
O
W
I
C
K
I

L
A
N
I
E
R

The main design objectives of the project were the preservation of the garden environment of the site by creating an architecture that is sympathetic to the landscape and the expression of ideas about the relationship of objects architecturally that were primarily inspired by our collaboration with the clients and readings of "Krazy Kat" comic strips. The architectural language is based on the associative meaning derived through juxtaposing symbolic elements. Similar elements were designed to express dissimilar qualities. Dissimilar elements were designed to express related qualities. They coexist to intensify the various aspects of interiority and exteriority (i.e., can one experience being within the garden and within an architectural enclosure at the same time?). The experience of the site extends this dialogue further by addressing two worlds simultaneously: the neighborhood/street and the garden. Both worlds are comprised of like elements. The world belonging to the neighborhood/street consists of a front yard, the existing house, and a rear garden deck bordered by a pool. It is joined by a bridge over the pool to the world of the garden: the guesthouse, a lower garden, and a creek.

The guesthouse is composed of two major elements with a connecting piece between. The two elements are the living room and the bedroom. The link between the two rooms is a dining area and table. An earthen stair forms the roof above and joins the pool deck to the lower garden.

O'Neill Residence: Barn,
West Los Angeles, California,1988.
Black & white source photograph.

O'Neill Residence: Bunker, *1989.*
Black & white source photograph.

O'Neill Guesthouse, *West Los Angeles, California, 1989.*
Plan and Elevations. Ink on paper,
24 1/8 x 15 11/16 in
(61 x 39 cm).

O'Neill Guesthouse, 1989.
Site Plan and Longitudinal Section.
Ink on paper,
24 1/8 x 15 11/16 in
(61 x 39 cm).

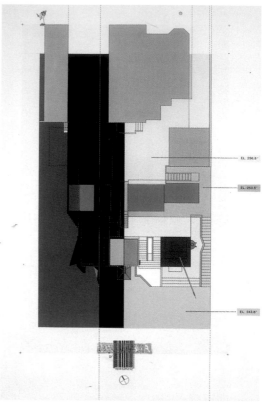

O'Neill Guesthouse, *1989.*
Cross Sections. Ink on paper,
24 1/8 x 15 11/16 in (61 x 39 cm).

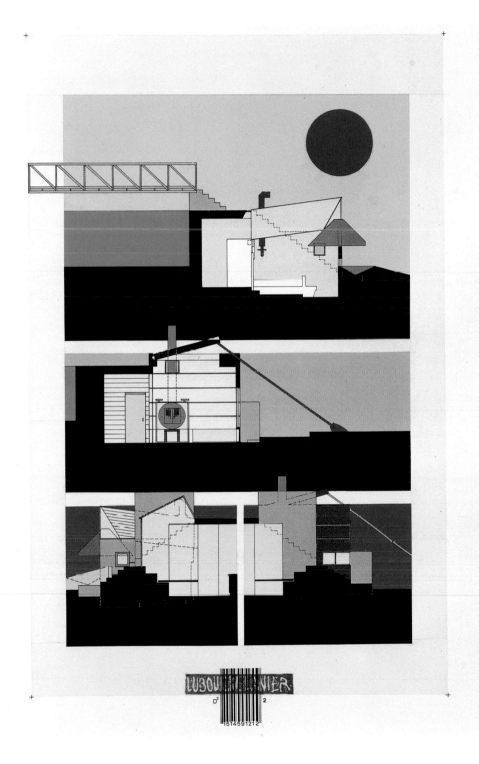

O'Neill Guesthouse: Four
Perspectives, *1989.*
*East, West, Northwest, and
Southwest Elevations. Model. Wood,
museum board, and foamcore,
35 3/8 x 25 x 10 in
(90 x 64 x 25 cm).*

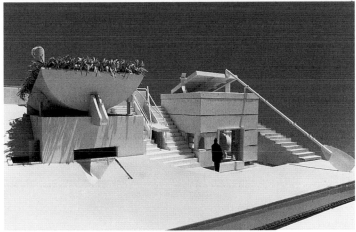

O'Neill Guesthouse, *1989.*
Model. Wood, museum board, and
foamcore,
57 1/4 x 12 3/4 x 12 in
(145 x 32 x 30 cm).

Berlin: Monument or Model for the Future? Allotment Garden City and Fishing Settlement

M
A
R
K

M
A
C
K

From the airplane, one perceives the Berlin Wall not as an urban tool of separation but as a rural void. Two-thirds of the wall pass through landscape and agricultural land. Barbed wire fences, sometimes several layers thick, and a controlled no man's land, make this wall a dramatic incision into the landscapes around Berlin. In the creation of this no man's land, hundreds of small garden and weekend houses were razed, and thousands of allotment gardens were nullified. Fifteen-meter-high sentry towers were erected at strategic locations and landmines rendered these former recreational areas obsolete.

Taking this lost land as a generative idea, this project recalls the spirit of turn-of-the-century Berlin, when the city was engaged in radical urban and land planning, a movement that was sober yet emotional. It revives the memory of the garden city movement under Hermann von Muthesius, the concepts of Martin Wagner, and the emotional socialism of Bruno Taut. The project is dedicated to this period of optimism and neighborly love and its outstanding architectural heroes.

Extraterritorial areas now located within East Berlin are connected back to West Berlin. These pedestrian enclaves, accessible by train, boat, or foot, provide an alternative to the urban bustle of the inner city. Tunnels, ramps, and catwalks bridge the small distance that separates these areas from the West. Over-scaled fences articulate the wall which support lean-to housing. These pockets of development are designed for those who still crave small-scale living.

Berlin: Monument or Model for
the Future?, *1988.*
*Perspective. Ink on bristol board,
8 1/4 x 11 1/2 in (21 x 29 cm).*

Berlin: Monument or Model for
the Future?, *1988.*
Site Plan and Elevations. Ink,
watercolor, and airbrush on
bristol board,
40 x 30 in (102 x 76 cm).

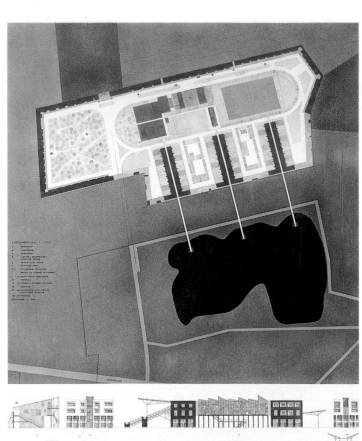

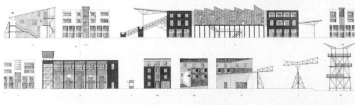

Berlin: Monument or Model
for the Future?, *1988.*
Perspective. Watercolor and
airbrush on photocopy,
15 1/2 x 10 3/4 in (39 x 27 cm).

Berlin: Monument or Model
for the Future?, 1988.
Plans, Sections, Elevations.
Photostat composite,
17 1/2 x 34 3/4 in
(44 x 88 cm).

Berlin: Monument or Model for
the Future?, 1988.
Axonometric sketch, section.
Ink on vellum,
8 x 11 1/2 in (21 x 29 cm).

M
A
R
K

M
A
C
K

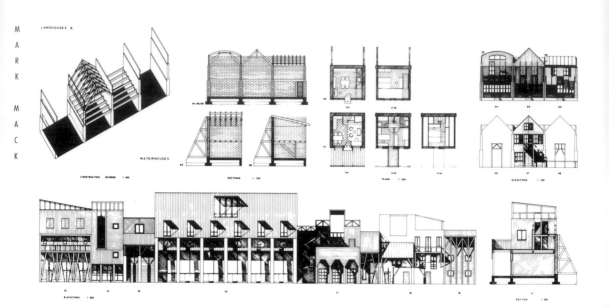

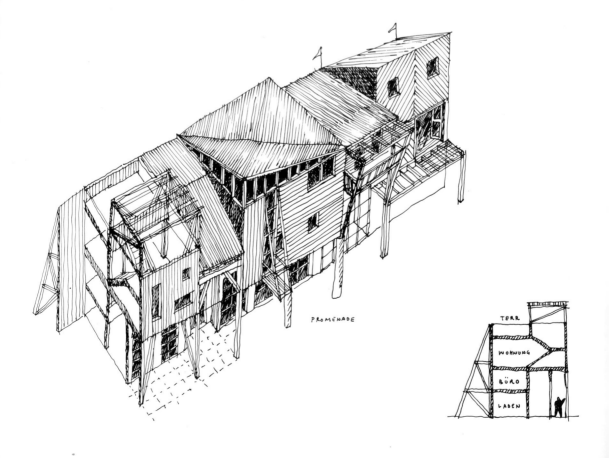

PROMENADE

TERR
WOHNUNG
BÜRO
LADEN

Berlin: Monument or Model for the Future?, *1988.*
Axonometric sketch, section. Ink on vellum,
11 1/2 x 8 1/4 in (29 x 21 cm).

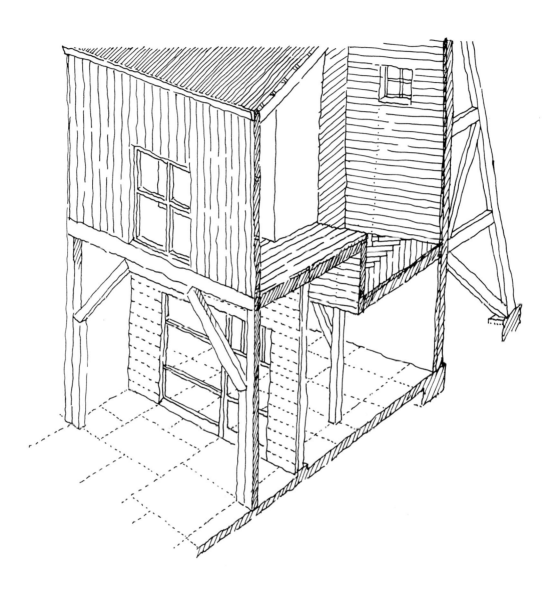

ARKADEN IM SCHREBERGARTEN   FICHTENWIESE BERLIN 88

Berlin: Monument or Model
for the Future?, *1988.*
*Perspective. Ink, watercolor,
and airbrush on bristol board,
20 x 14 in (51x 36 cm).*

Berlin: Monument or Model for
the Future?, *1988.*
*Perspective. Watercolor and airbrush
on photocopy,
10 3/4 x 16 1/2 in (27 x 42 cm).*

Sixth Street House

Barking Dog and Dancing Angel

The Sixth Street House project continues our investigation of the impacted or imploded building, a metaphor for the veils or walls with which we protect ourselves from the world and from the secrets and mysteries that are so much a part of the human condition. As part of the diffused Los Angeles metropolis, this project accepts the suburban context as a point of departure. Present are the traditional concerns of shelter, structure, use, materiality, order, beauty, and meaning.

The Sixth Street House is about objects and buildings, the one self-sufficient and uninhabitable, and the other integrated, accommodating, and occupiable. The invention and importation of ten pieces, whose original purpose has been lost, brings to the sight an imagined prehistory—a contemporary archaeology. The work prompts doubts about the impersonal and detached existence of things.

The house explores the ground between these ten found objects and the building. The pieces (parts of discarded machinery or dead tech) impart decay, tension, risk, balance—a world between utopia and atopia. Manipulated independently, simultaneously separated and associated through a geometric order, these discrete pieces describe a vision of a world that is neither fragmented nor whole.

Beauty and ugliness blur.

This work is done with the awareness that one's personal sensibility could have been otherwise.

Barking Dog and Dancing Angel are two of a series of pieces that were conceived in response to the ten embedded objects that form the dialogue of the Sixth Street House project. Similar to the embedded constructions, these "light objects" question the mechanical nature of our world with its aspiration for an architecture that optimizes technology. Both lack any direct interest in the priority with more personalized intentions for machinery's use. They share an interest in containing and directing light (and energy). Both objects are interactive and allow for an engagement with their human partners. The angel light has three modes of intensity activated by stroking; the dog (or guard light) senses one's movement by infrared light and by sound. It is not unusual to see children as well as adults attempting to escape detection—darting this way and that, crouching low, and then down on all fours.

Sixth Street House, *Los Angeles,*
California, 1988. Composite.
Serigraph on Arches 88 paper,
40 x 30 in (102 x 76 cm).

Following page
Barking Dog, *1986.*
Prototype. Aluminum and
corten steel,
39 x 20 x 6 1/2 in
(99 x 51 x 17 cm).

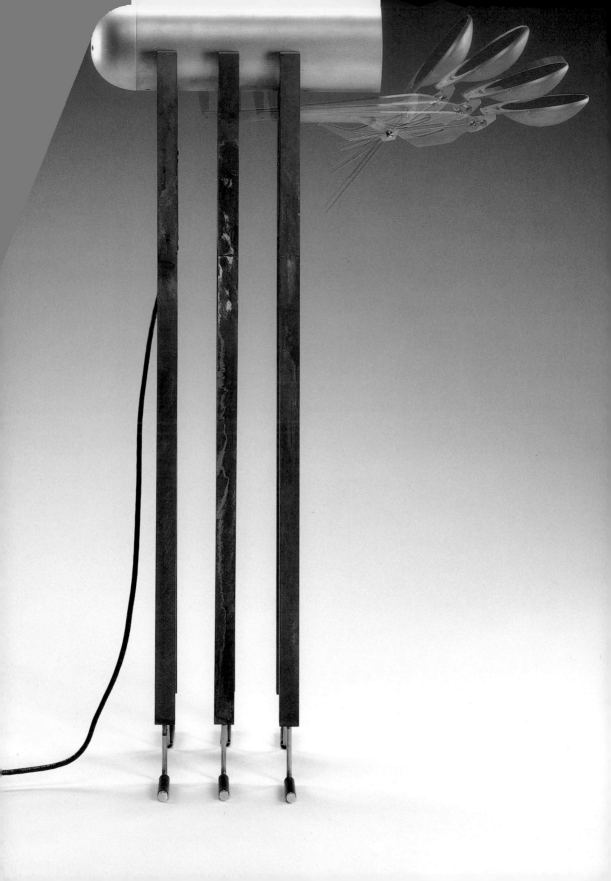

Preceding page
Dancing Angel, *1988.*
Prototype. Stainless, corten, and carbon steel,
70 x 14 x 7 in (178 x 36 x18 cm).

Sixth Street House: Fig. 2, *1988.*
North-South Section. Ink and
graphite on Strathmore board,
40 x 30 in (102 x 76 cm).

T
H
O
M

M
A
Y
N
E

M
O
R
P
H
O
S
I
S

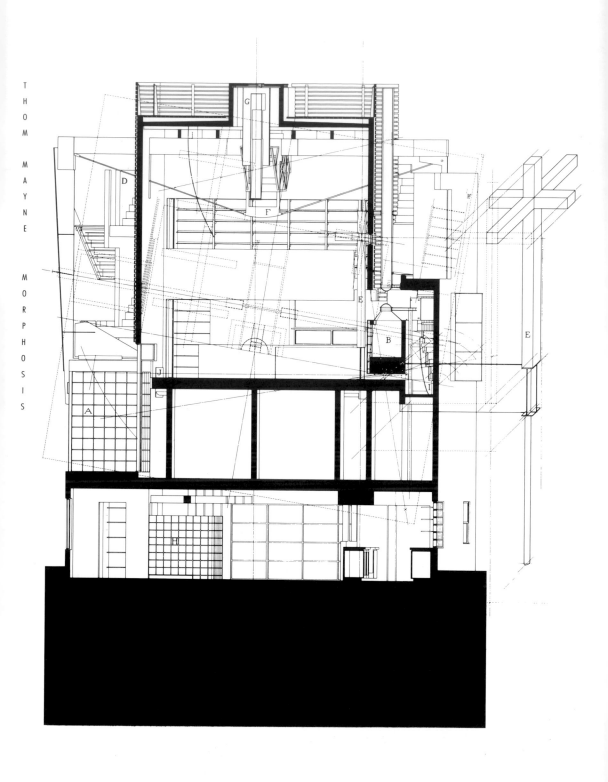

Sixth Street House: Fig. 10, *1988.*
East-West Section. Ink and graphite
on Strathmore board,
40 x 30 in (76 x 102 cm).

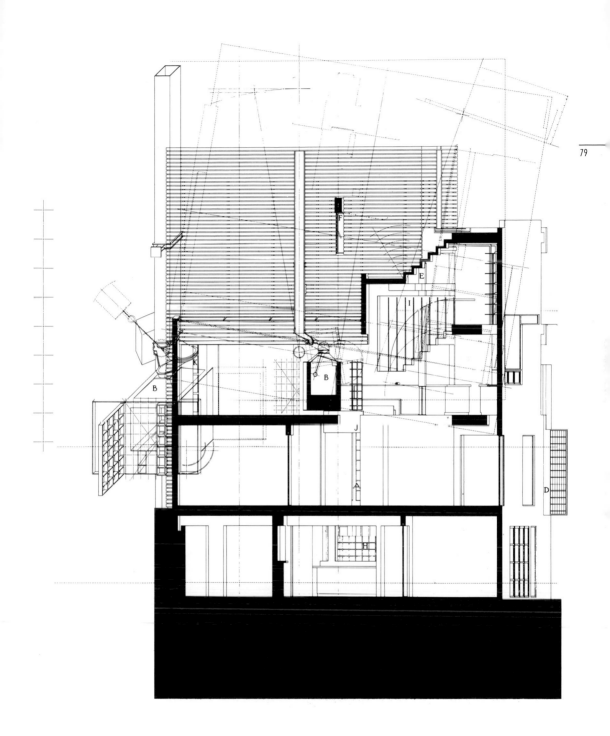

Sixth Street House, *1988.*
Model looking west.

Sixth Street House, *1988.*
Model looking east. Acrylic,
modeling paste, chipboard,
and foamcore,
16 x 16 x 27 in
(41 x 41 x 69 cm).
Steel base,
16 x 16 x 36 in
(41 x 41 x 91 cm).

S.P.A.R.CITY
(Southern Pacific Air Rights City)
Nara Convention Center

E
R
I
C

O
W
E
N

M
O
S
S

CLX.

Out of
place is
the one
right place.

> *Moss Herbert*
> Small Immensities

An abandoned Southern Pacific Railroad right of way arcs one-half mile from the Los Angeles River to National Boulevard. The old tracks run through what for fifty years has been a light industrial/manufacturing area. The form of the project varies over its length as it extends, amends, contradicts, and reconfirms uses that adjoin the right of way. Two personalities exist for buildings that adjoin the right of way: friendly and unfriendly. If a building is friendly, it can open to the right of way and the air-rights construction can abut, lean on, or extend over the existing building. This suggests a series of new/rehabilitated, restored/reconstructed industrial structures along the line.

If the adjacency is unfriendly, new air-rights structures simply pass by. Existing structures continue to operate, with access from adjacent streets. If adjacent properties are vacant the S.P.A.R.C I T Y structure extends perpendicularly to itself, expropriating new territory. The plan is egalitarian and totalitarian. It adds to existing uses; it subtracts others; it entices; it compels.

" . . . the great globe itself,
Yea all which it inherit, shall dissolve. . . .
And like this unsubstantial pageant faded,
Leave not a rack behind."

> The Tempest, IV, 1

The Nara Convention Center has three components—Plaza Building (earth), Roof Building (sky), and Theater Building (bridge between)—each of which has both organizational and philosophical roles in the project concept.

The site—the Plaza Building—is conceived as an open-air multipurpose plaza and garden. The plaza will include a commemoration of the 1300-year-old Buddhist origins of Nara, and will be carved into the earth, offering several levels of walks and gardens.

The Roof Building, raised above the plaza, contains a two-level, four-way pedestrian street, a theoretical extension of the city grid. The grid suggests a reconnected movement system uniting the Convention Center, the redevelopment site, and the old city.

The Theater Buildings, raised on legs, form a conceptual and physical bridge between the Roof and Plaza Buildings. The theater structure

Nara Convention Center,
Nara, Japan, 1991.
Red and black ink on card stock,
11 x 8 1/2 in (28 x 22 cm).

originates as a parabolic curve, derived from the optimal viewing angle.

Symbolically, the roof (a portion of a globe) is a primitive, idealized form of both earth and sky. The building is a theoretical sphere. But the sphere is modified to accommodate the specifics of the city, the program, and the site. Thus the project is simultaneously theoretical and pragmatic.

The top of the globe is the curved roof form. The top of the top is cut off. The circular plan of the globe appears only where it crosses the southeast corner of the site. The theoretical perimeter of the circle as it traverses the city beyond the Convention Center site defines a hypothetical limit for extending the grid in the air. Nara Convention Center's three pieces form, and are formed by, the dissolving globe which will move Nara past the past, into the future.

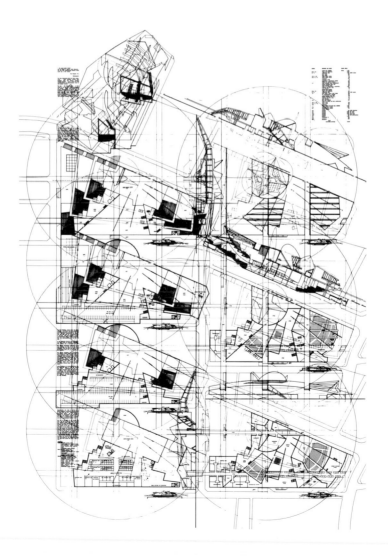

Nara Convention Center, *1991.*
Model. Strathmore board, modeling
paste, bass wood, foamcore, and
wire mesh,
33 x 23 1/2 in
(84 x 60 cm).

Nara Convention Center, *1991.*
Model. Strathmore board, modeling
paste, bass wood, foamcore, and
wire mesh,
24 x 16 1/2 in
(61 x 42 cm).

Nara Convention Center, *1991.*
Model. Strathmore board, modeling
paste, bass wood, foamcore, and
wire mesh,
24 x 16 1/2 in (61 x 42 cm).

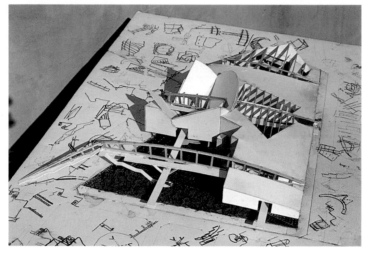

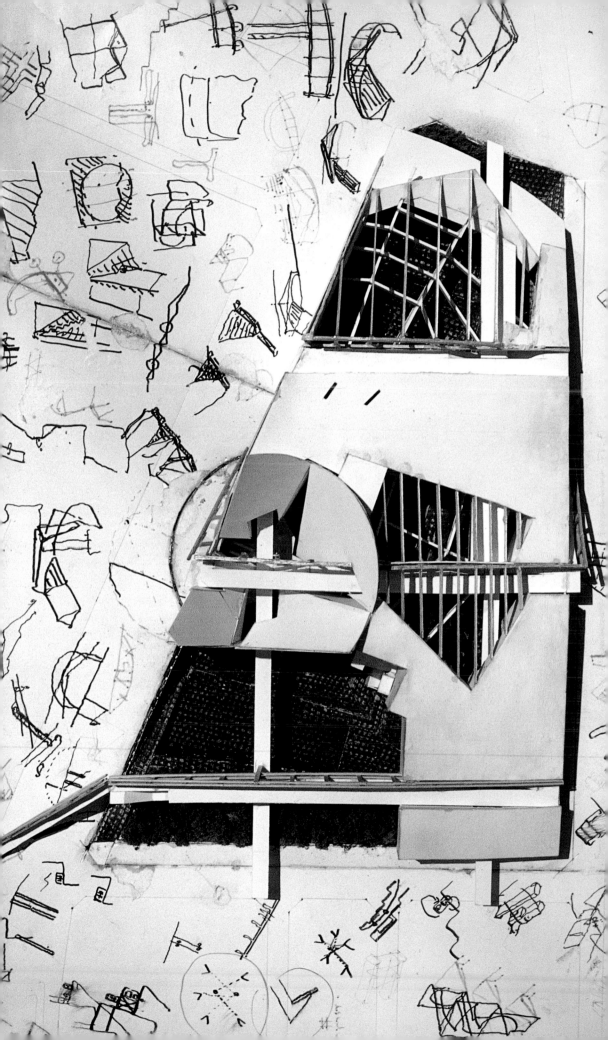

Nara Convention Center,
1991.
*Red and black ink on card
stock,*
11 x 8 1/2 in (28 x 22 cm).

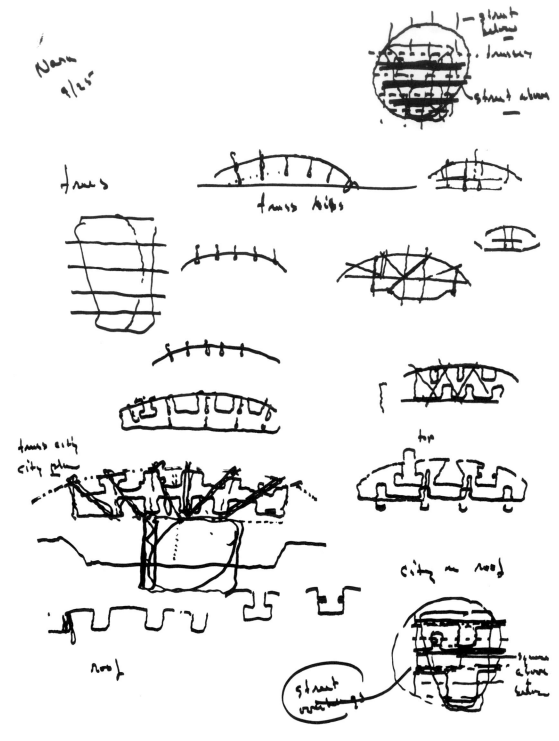

Nara Convention Center, *1991.*
Black & white composite photograph,
42 x 56 in (107 x 142 cm).

S.P.A.R.C I T Y: Concourse,
Los Angeles, California, 1991—.
Diazo blueline print,
22 x 17 in (56 x 43 cm).

S.P.A.R.C I T Y : Hayden Bridge,
1991—.
Diazo blueline print,
21 x 17 in (53 x 43 cm).

S.P.A.R.C I T Y : Eastham Bridge,
1991—.
Diazo blueline print, 21 1/2 x 16 in
(55 x 41 cm).

S.P.A.R.C I T Y : Site, 1991—.
Diazo blueline print,
22 x 17 in (56 x 43 cm).

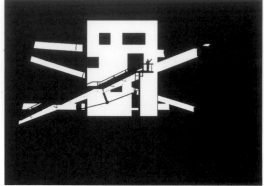

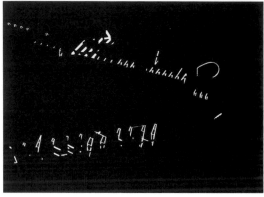

S.P.A.R.C I T Y: Riverwalk,
1991—.
Diazo blueline print,
16 x 21 1/2 in (41 x 55 cm).

S.P.A.R.C I T Y : Hayden Bridge,
1991—.
Diazo blueline print,
22 x 17 in (56 x 43 cm).

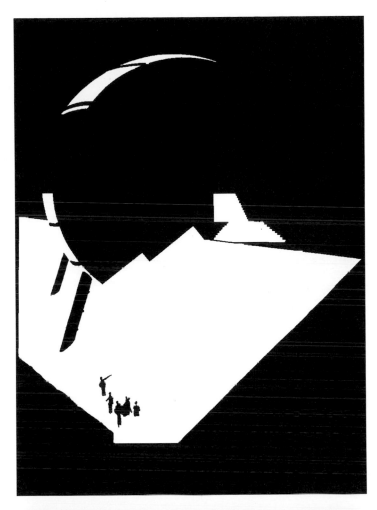

Mill Race Park

S
T
A
N
L
E
Y

S
A
I
T
O
W
I
T
Z

The quality of the city of Columbus should be reflected in the park. In the way that a tree inhabits the city, remembering nature, the structures inhabit the park, remembering the city.

The group of buildings in the park is conceived of as a family, each with the same genes, derived from the same geometry, speaking a common language. The family is divided into genders, one having the characteristics of use specificity, where program informs form; the other, the characteristics of site specificity, where amplifying the site is the formal generator.

The genetic structure of the buildings revolves around an architecture of roofs as primal in shelter making: roofs as fragments of the dome of sky, cut by forms which emerge as plan on the ground. Each structure presents a gesture of singularity which aims to create an object of definite ambiguity. All structures arise from similar geometries—squares intersecting circles—interpreted specifically in relation to site or program. All are made of concrete ground structures with steel roofs, some corrugated, some perforated, and supported by steel tubes.

The nine park structures concretize their situational reality. They amplify the site; they proclaim their functions publicly.

Mill Race Park, *Columbus,*
Indiana, 1991.
Site plan. Ink on mylar,
24 x 36 in (61 x 91 cm).

Mill Race Park, *1991. Site.*

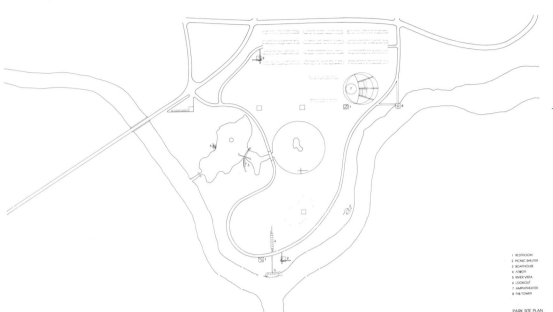

1. RESTROOM
2. PICNIC SHELTER
3. BOATHOUSE
4. ARBOR
5. RIVER VISTA
6. LOOKOUT
7. AMPHITHEATER
8. THE TOWER

PARK SITE PLAN

Mill Race Park: Large Picnic
Shelter, *1991.*
Model. Wood and metal,
9 x 9 x 3 in (23 x 23 x 8 cm).

Mill Race Park: Boathouse, *1991.*
Model. Wood, metal, styrene, and
plastic,
12 x 24 x 3 in (30 x 61 x 8 cm).

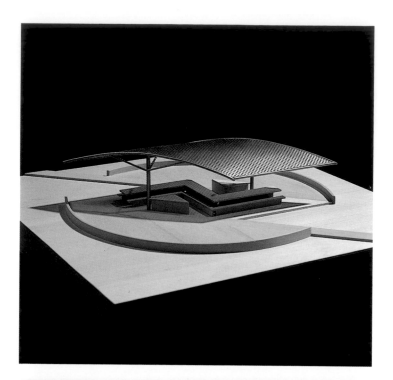

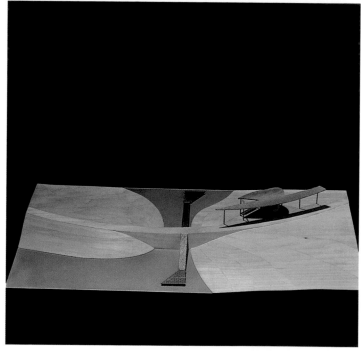

Mill Race Park: Restrooms, *1991.*
Model. Wood, styrene, and plastic,
6 x 6 x 3 in (15 x 15 x 8 cm).

Mill Race Park: Small Picnic
Shelter, *1991.*
Model. Wood and metal,
6 x 6 x 3 in (15 x 15 x 8 cm).

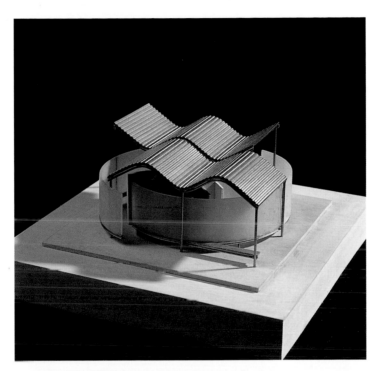

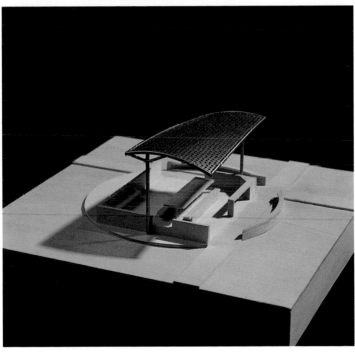

Mill Race Park, *1991.*
Ink on mylar,
24 x 36 in (61 x 91 cm).
Tower
Large Restroom
Picnic Shelter
Small Picnic Shelter
Amphitheater

S
T
A
N
L
E
Y

S
A
I
T
O
W
I
T
Z

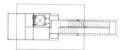

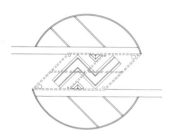

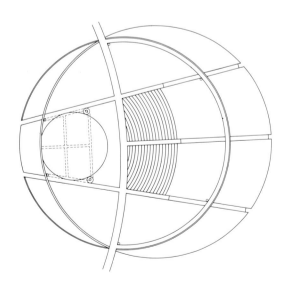

Mill Race Park, *1991.*
Ink on mylar,
24 x 36 in (61 x 91 cm).
Boathouse
Arbor
River Vista
Lookout
Stage

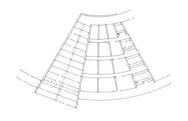

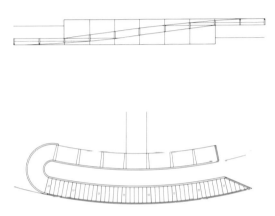

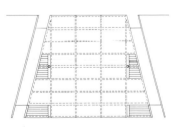

Mill Race Park: Arbor, *1991.*
Model. Wood and metal,
6 x 18 x 3 in (15 x 46 x 8 cm).

Mill Race Park: River Vista, *1991.*
Model. Wood, metal, and styrene,
9 x 24 x 3 in (23 x 61 x 8 cm).

Mill Race Park: Lookout, *1991.*
Model. Wood, metal, and styrene,
9 x 9 x 3 in (23 x 23 x 8 cm).

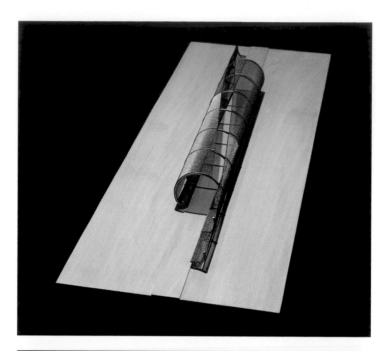

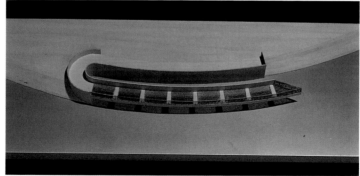

Mill Race Park: Amphitheater,
1991.
Model. Wood, 18 x 18 x 3 in
(46 x 46 x 8 cm).

Mill Race Park: Tower, *1991.*
Model. Wood, metal, and styrene,
6 x 6 x 12 in
(15 x 15 x 30 cm).

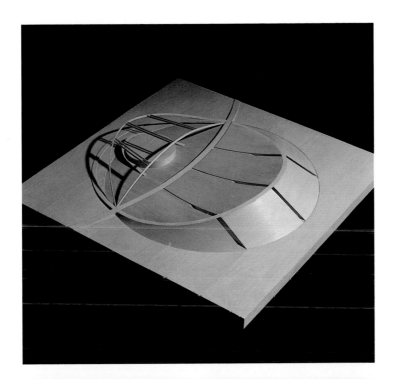

The Archaeology of Furniture: Drawings from Giotto

Giotto lived seven hundred years ago, from 1267 to 1337. His work is revolutionary in its depiction of the human figure. Of equal interest to us is his depiction of buildings and furniture. Giotto's medieval city is a composition of multicolored buildings, not the monochrome present reality. The buildings and furniture are simple in form, but are powerfully evocative. They often seem like people, and are active participants in the telling of stories.

In "Drawings from Giotto," we have made three-dimensional drawings of some of the furniture that exists in the reality of Giotto's paintings. Our furniture, then, is a depiction of another reality. The pieces can also be seen, almost by accident, as furniture to be used. We imagine their use by both body and mind in ways other than those specified by their names.

Bed: The cure of the man from Ilerda

A saint heals a man with leprosy in soul and body. The repentant man dies fifteen days later and appears to the saint in a vision, thanking him for the cure on his way to paradise. The long narrow wooden bed with its white sheet is a place for thinking about being cured, or thinking about what requires curing. The blue of the pillow comes from the sky in the painting. The bed is also a place for thinking about paradise.

Chest: Annunciation to St. Anne

A saint, while praying, is told by an angel that she is to be mother of a virgin who will bear a child. The simple room is crowded with the fundamentals of furniture—a bed with accompanying bench, a canopy for protecting the bed place, and a chest for containing clothing and other personal articles. The red iron oxide chest can be seen as an empty box to house space (the color inside taken from the sky in the painting), free from the crowding of artifacts that seems required to support modern life.

Canopy: St. Francis sees in a dream a palace filled with arms

In a dream, a saint is shown a great and splendid palace with armaments, a symbol of the Franciscan "army" of the future. The four-posted structure at the left of the painting is both the place for the saint's bed and the room itself. The yellow ochre canopy, then, is a place for having a vision of an idea and a mechanism for transforming the present. One curtain (behind) simply hangs from the round bar; the other (ahead) is tied around the square column of the canopy. The structure rests on a platform—the frame of the painting and the threshold to a place for seeing the future in a dream.

(Robert Mangurian and Mary-Ann Ray)

The Archaeology of Furniture:
Crucifix, *1991.*
Auto body putty on wood,
91 x 64 x 18 in
(231 x 162 x 46 cm).

Giotto. S. Francesco celebra
il Natale a Greccio allestendo il
primo Presepio (St. Francis
celebrates Christmas and his first
crib in Greccio), *after 1296.*
Fresco.
Upper Church, Assisi.

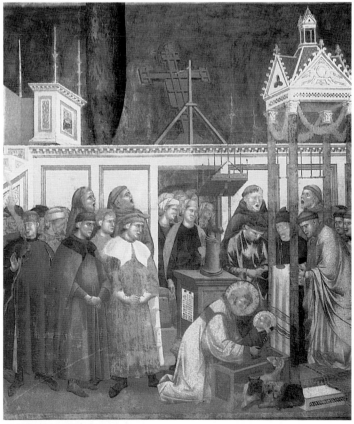

The Archaeology of Furniture:
Bed, *1991.*
Graphite and prismacolor on paper,
11 x 17 in (28 x 43 cm).

Giotto. La Guarigione dell'Uomo
di Ilerda (The cure of the man
from Ilerda),
after 1296. Fresco.
Upper Church, Assisi.

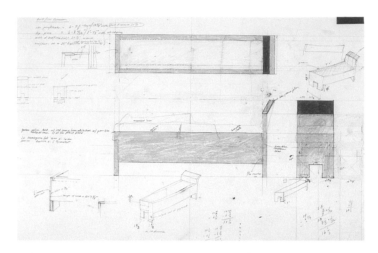

The Archaeology of Furniture:
Bed, *1991.*
Maquette. Pigment in plaster on
wood,
46 x 20 1/4 x 87 1/2 in
(117 x 51 x 222 cm).

The Archaeology of Furniture:
Chest, *1991.*
*Graphite and prismacolor on
paper,
7 3/16 x 11 in (18 x 28 cm).*

Giotto. L'Annunzio a S. Anna
(Annunciation to St. Anne),
*after 1304. Fresco.
The Arena Chapel, Padua.*

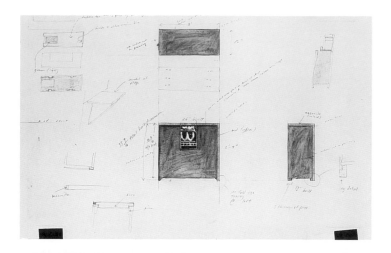

The Archaeology of Furniture:
Chest, *1991*.
*Maquette. Pigment in plaster on
wood,*
33 1/2 x 36 x 12 in
(85 x 91 x 30 cm).

The Archaeology of Furniture:
Canopy, *1991. Graphite and
prismacolor on paper,
7 3/16 x 11 in (18 x 28 cm).*

Giotto. S. Francesco vede nel Sogno
un Palazzo pieno d'Armi
(St. Francis sees in a dream a palace
filled with arms),
*after 1296. Fresco.
Upper Church, Assisi.*

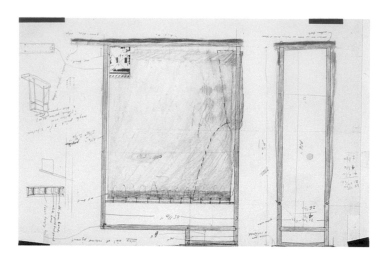

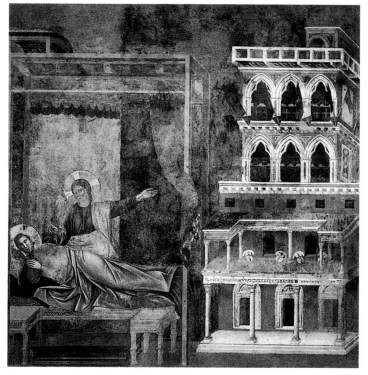

The Archaeology of Furniture:
Canopy, *1991.*
*Maquette. Pigment in plaster on
wood,
114 1/2 x 26 x 85 3/4 in
(218 x 66 x 291 cm).*

Details

Holt Hinshaw Pfau Jones
Paramount Film and Tape Archive,
Hollywood, California, 1990.
Upper entryway.
Concrete structure, steel, and plaster.

Frank Israel
Bright and Associates,
Venice, California, 1990.
Conference room.
Birch plywood, bonderized sheet
metal door.

Craig Hodgetts & Hsin-Ming Fung
Hemdale Film Corporation,
Los Angeles, California,
1989–90.
Atrium. Wood and aluminum.

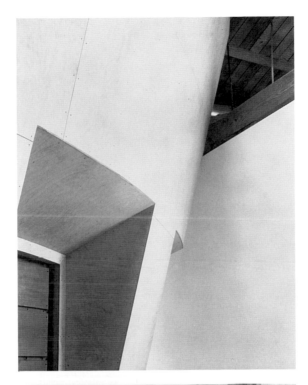

Mark Mack
Summers Residence,
Santa Monica, California, 1990.
Exterior, towards terrace.
Stucco, wood siding, concrete block.

Thom Mayne, Morphosis
Crawford Residence,
Montecito, California, 1990.
Raw steel and aluminum (chair);
redwood exterior.

Lubowicki Lanier
NANA Trading Co.,
Santa Monica, California, 1991.
Men's Dressing Room.
Stained particle board.

Koning Eizenberg
Santa Monica House,
Santa Monica, California, 1989.
Entry. Cedar, glass, stucco.

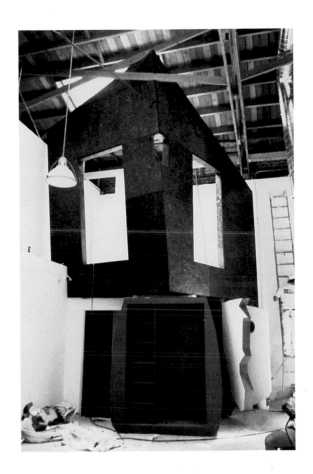

Stanley Saitowitz
California Museum of
Photography,
Riverside, California, 1990.
Stair and elevator. Steel,
perforated metal, and woven wire.

D
E
T
A
I
L
S

Eric Owen Moss
8522 National,
Culver City, California, 1990.
Elliptical entry court. Existing
timber structure, steel, sheet metal.

Studio Works
Southside Settlement,
Columbus, Ohio, 1980.
Wall detail. Cab board.

Frank O. Gehry & Associates, Inc.

Frank Gehry   Born 1929; Toronto, Canada

Education
University of Southern California
Harvard University Graduate School of Design

Awards
The William Bishop Chair, Yale University School of Architecture, 1979
Pritzker Prize for Architecture, 1989
Arnold W. Brunner Memorial Prize in Architecture, 1989
American Institute of Architects Los Angeles Chapter Honor Award,
            Edgemar Development, Santa Monica, California, 1989
Gold Medal, American Institute of Architects Los Angeles Chapter, 1989
Furniture Manufacturing and Design Museum, Weil am Rhein, Germany, 1990
American Institute of Architects Southern California Chapter Design Award,
            Chiat/Day Advertising, Toronto, Canada, 1990
American Institute of Architects Honor Award, Schnabel Residence,
            Brentwood, California, 1990
Connecticut Society of Architects Honor Award, Yale Psychiatric Institute,
            New Haven, Connecticut, 1991
Progressive Architecture Award, The American Center in Paris, 1991
American Institute of Architects Los Angeles Chapter Honor Award, Vitra Honor
            Award, Chiat Day Main Street, Venice, California, 1992
Wolf Prize in Arts (Architecture), 1992

Academic Affiliations
Assistant Professor, University of California, 1972–73
Instructor, Southern California Institute of Architecture, 1975–76
Visiting Critic, Rice University, Houston, Texas, 1976
Visiting Critic, University of California at Los Angeles, 1977, 1979
Visiting Critic, Harvard University Graduate School of Design, 1983
Assistant Professor, University of California at Los Angeles, 1989
Advisory Council, Princeton University School of Architecture, 1991
Visiting Committee, Harvard University Graduate School of Design, 1991–92
Sir Banister Fletcher Visiting Professorship, Bartlett School of Architecture and
            Planning, 1992

Publications
Frank Gehry, Buildings and Projects. Peter Arnell and Ted Bickford, eds.
            New York: Rizzoli, 1985.
The Architecture of Frank Gehry. Foreword by Henry N.Cobb. Essays by
            Rosemarie Haag Bletter, et al. New York: Rizzoli, 1986.

Craig Hodgetts & Hsin-Ming Fung

Craig Hodgetts   Born 1937; Cincinnati, Ohio

Education
General Motors Institute, 1956
Oberlin College, 1958
San Francisco State University, 1960
Yale University, 1967

Awards
Eero Saarinen Memorial Award, Yale University, 1966
Progressive Architecture Awards and Citations, 1969, 1972, 1976
Meritorious Award, West Hollywood Civic Center Design Competition,
          Los Angeles, California, 1987
First Award, Los Angeles Arts Park International Design Competition, 1989
Special Commendation, Blueprints for Modern Living Exhibition, Museum of
          Contemporary Art, Los Angeles, California, 1990

Academic Affiliations
Adjunct Associate Professor, University of Pennsylvania School of Architecture,
          1980–present
Visiting Critic, Southern California Institute of Architecture, 1987–present
Professor, Graduate School of Architecture and Urban Design, University of
          California at San Diego, 1991–present

Professional Affiliations
James Stirling and Associates, New York, 1967–1969
Studio Works, Venice, California, 1969–1984

Exhibitions
The New Urban Landscape, World Financial Center, New York, 1988
Blueprints for Modern Living, Museum of Contemporary Art, Los Angeles, 1989
Franklin/La Brea Low Income Housing, Museum of Contemporary Art,
          Los Angeles, 1989
Visionary San Francisco, San Francisco Museum of Modern Art, 1990

Projects
Gateway, University of California at Los Angeles
C.S.I. Production Facilities, Los Angeles, California
Thames Residence, Los Angeles, California
Walt Disney Imagineering, Tokyo and Paris

Publications
Progressive Architecture, May 1988, October 1988, September 1990
Domus, December 1989
Art in America, March 1990

Holt Hinshaw Pfau Jones Architecture

Founded

Marc Hinshaw and Paul Holt, 1980; Peter Pfau and Wes Jones, 1987

Education

The principals hold degrees from the Harvard University Graduate School of
Design, the University of Manchester, United Kingdom, Columbia University,
and the University of California, Berkeley.

Awards

Rome Prize in Architecture, 1985–86; Wes Jones
Progressive Architecture Awards, 1987, 1989
Finalist, Invited Competition for U.S. Pavilion, EXPO 92, 1989
Winner, Invited Competition, University of California at Los Angeles, 1989
Progressive Architecture Citations, 1990, 1991
Finalist, Rene Dubos Bioshelter Competition, New York, 1991

Exhibitions

AIA Conference on Homelessness, Washington, D.C., 1985
Building Machines, Institute for Art and Urban Resources (PS 1),
New York, 1986
Installed Mechanisms, Graduate School of Architecture,
Columbia University, 1987
California Lifeguard Towers, Kirsten Kiser Gallery, 1988
The Outdoor Chair Show, Sausalito, California, 1987
Communicating Ideas Artfully, Steelcase Design Partnership, 1990

Projects

Astronaut's Memorial, Kennedy Space Center, 1991
Paramount Pictures Film and Tape Archives, Hollywood, California, 1991

Publications

New York Times, 1986
Architecture and Urbanism, 1986
Transitions: Discourse on Architecture, Vol. 4, No. 3 (1986)
Progressive Architecture, 1987, 1988, 1989, 1991
Art Forum, 1987
Interior Design, 1987
New Architecture San Francisco, 1989
The Architecture Review, 1989
Architecture in Perspective IV, 1989
Architectural Drawing, 1990
Metropolitan Home, 1990

Franklin D. Israel Design Associates Inc.

Frank Israel   Born 1945; New York, New York

Education
Penn State
Yale University
Columbia University

Awards
Lucilee Snyster Memorial Award, Columbia University, 1971
A.I.A. Gold Medal, Columbia University, 1971
Rome Prize, American Academy in Rome, 1973–1975
Progressive Architecture Citation, 1977
Architectural League Award, 1977

Academic Affiliations
Associate Professor, Harvard University Graduate School of Design
Associate Professor of Architecture, Graduate School of Architecture and Urban
               Planning, University of California, Los Angeles

Professional Affiliations
Giovanni Pasanella, New York
Llewellyn-Davies, Weeks, Forestier-Walker and Bor, London and Teheran

Exhibitions
Architecture Tomorrow: Franklin D. Israel, Walker Art Gallery, Minneapolis;
               San Francisco Museum of Art; Murray Feldman Gallery,
               Los Angeles, 1988
From Cities Within, American Institute of Architects Dallas Chapter, 1990
Drawings, Getty Center, Santa Monica, California, 1990–91
Les Architectes Plasticiens, Saddock and Uzzan Gallery, Paris, 1991

Projects
Propaganda Films, Hollywood
Tisch/Avnet Productions, Los Angeles
Bright & Assoc, Venice, California
Altman Beach House, Malibu, California

Publications
New York Times Magazine, April 22, 1990
Architectural Digest, A.D. 100, August 15, 1991
G.A. Houses, Volumes 30 and 31, 1991
Architectural Record, February 1992

Koning Eizenberg Architecture

Julie Eizenberg   Born 1954; Melbourne, Australia

Education
University of Melbourne, Australia
University of California at Los Angeles

Academic Affiliations
Lecturer, Graduate School of Architecture and Urban Planning, University of
California at Los Angeles

Hendrik Koning   Born 1953; Melbourne, Australia

Education
University of Melbourne, Australia
University of California at Los Angeles

Koning Eizenberg

Awards
Progressive Architecture First Award, Affordable Housing, 1987
Architectural Record House, Hollywood Duplex, 1988
Top 30, Domino's Farms Activities, 1989
Westside Urban Forum Prize, Real Estate Development—Land Use Planning
            Urban Design: Farmers Market Historic Preservation, 1991
American Institute of Architects Los Angeles Chapter Award of Merit,
            909 House, 1991
Nell Norris Award, School of Architecture and Planning, University of
            Melbourne, 1991

Projects
Gilmore Bank, Los Angeles, current
Farmers Market, Los Angeles, current
Simone Hotel, Los Angeles, 1992
Ken Edwards Center for Community Services, 1991
Community Corporation of Santa Monica Housing Projects, Santa Monica, 1988
Liffman House, Santa Monica, 1988

Lubowicki Lanier

Paul Lubowicki   Born 1954; New Haven, Connecticut

Education
Cooper Union, 1977

Academic Affiliations
Faculty, Southern California Institute of Architecture

Professional Affiliations
Frank O. Gehry & Associates

Susan Lanier   Born 1949; Long Beach, California

Education
Pitzer College (Psychology), 1971
Southern California Institute of Architecture, 1988

Academic Affiliations
Faculty, Southern California Institute of Architecture

Professional Affiliations
Morphosis

Lubowicki Lanier

Projects
Nana Trading Company, Santa Monica, California
Prototype Bale Chair
Alden Custom Furniture, Pacific Palisades, California
Stringfellow Residential Addition, Hollywood Hills, California
Santa Monica Museum of Art Interior Renovation, Santa Monica, California
Engelauf Residence, Riverside, California
Cooder Remodel, Pacific Palisades, California
O'Neill Guesthouse, West Los Angeles, California
Teller & Weill Guesthouse, Hollywood Hills, California
Spiller Condominiums (two projects), Ocean Park, California

Publications
Terrazzo: Architecture & Design, Spring 1989
Experimental Architecture in Los Angeles. Introduction by Frank Gehry. Essays by
        Aaron Betsky, John Chase, and Leon Whiteson. New York:
        Rizzoli, 1991.

MACK Architects

Mark Mack   Born 1949; Judenburg, Austria

Education
Academy of Fine Arts, Vienna, Austria

Awards
Architectural Record Award for Excellence in Planning and Design, 1989
Progressive Architecture Citation, 1990
Top 30, Domino's Farms Activities, 1991

Academic Affiliations
Visiting Professor, Associate Professor, University of California at Berkeley,
        College of Environmental Design, 1986–present

Professional Affiliations
Steiger & Partners, Zurich
Atelier Hans Hollein, Vienna
Hausrucker and Emilio Ambasz, Inc., New York
Western Addition, founder
Archetype Magazine, co-founder and editor

Exhibitions
Architectural Adumbrations: The Sketchbook and Contemporary Practice,
        Getty Center for the History of Art and the Humanities,
        Santa Monica, 1990–91
Three at the Gallery, American Institute of Architects San Francisco
        Chapter, 1991

Projects
Candlestick Park, San Francisco, 1991
Samarec Offices, New York, 1991
Kashii District Housing, Fukuoka, Japan, 1991
Thompson Residence, Kent-Woodlands, California, 1991
Summers Residence, Santa Monica, California, 1990
Boise Museum of Art, Boise, Idaho, 1988

Publications
Fukuoka International Architects' Conference 1989, Fukuoka City, Japan
14 x Amerika-Gedenkbibliothek: Architects From the U.S. Planning For Berlin,
        1989, Berlin, West Germany
Art Against AIDS, 1989, Headlines Table
Berlin: Denkmal oder Denkmodell?, 1988, Kunsthalle, Berlin
From Table to Tablescape, 1988, 333 Gallery, Chicago
The Emerging Generation in U.S.A., 1987, GA Gallery, Tokyo
Modern Redux, 1986, Grey Art Gallery, New York University
Forty under Forty, Interiors, 1986
Art, Architecture, & Landscape, 1985, San Francisco Museum of Modern Art

Thom Mayne, Morphosis

B
I
O
G
R
A
P
H
I
E
S

Thom Mayne   Born 1944; Waterbury, Connecticut

Education

University of Southern California School of Architecture

Harvard University Graduate School of Design

Awards

Progressive Architecture Awards and Citations, 1974, 1977, 1980, 1982, 1984, 1985, 1987, 1988, 1989, 1991

American Institute of Architects Awards, 1981, 1985, 1986, 1987, 1988, 1990, 1991

American Institute of Architects California Chapter Awards, 1986, 1988, 1989, 1990, 1992

Rome Prize Fellowship, 1987

American Academy of Arts and Letters, 1992

Academic Affiliations

Faculty, Founding Board Member, Southern California Institute of Architecture

Visiting Faculty, University of Illinois, Plym Chair, 1992

Visiting Faculty, Yale University, Eliel Saarinen Chair, 1991

Visiting Faculty, Academy of Applied Arts, Vienna, 1991

Visiting Faculty, Clemson University, Visiting Master Teacher, 1991

Visiting Faculty, University of Cincinnati, 1990

Visiting Faculty, Harvard University, Elliot Noyes Chair, 1988

Exhibitions

Laguna Art Museum, Laguna, California

San Francisco Museum of Modern Art, San Francisco

Contemporary Arts Center, Cincinnati, Ohio

Walker Arts Center, Minneapolis, Minnesota

Cheney Cowles Museum, Spokane, Washington

Cooper-Hewitt Museum, New York

Architectural Association, London

Institute of Contemporary Arts, London

California Museum of Science and Industry

Max Protetch Gallery, New York

Australian Center for Contemporary Art, Victoria, Australia

Publications

Morphosis, Buildings and Projects. Essays by Peter Cook and George Rand. New York: Rizzoli, 1989.

Thom Mayne, Sixth Street House. Edited by George Wagner. Cambridge: Harvard University Graduate School of Design, 1989.

Eric Owen Moss Architect

Eric Owen Moss   Born 1943; Brooklyn, New York

Education
University of California at Los Angeles
University of California at Berkeley, College of Environmental Design
Harvard University Graduate School of Design

Awards
American Institute of Architects Interior Design Awards of Excellence, 1992
Progressive Architecture Awards, 1992
American Institute of Architects California Council Urban Design Award,
        1981, 1986, 1988, 1991
American Institute of Architects Los Angeles Chapter Honor Awards,
        1977, 1979, 1983 (2), 1988, 1990, 1991

Academic Affiliations
Professor of Design, Director, Southern California Institute of Architecture

Exhibitions
Architectural Design: Theory and Experimentation, Symposium/Exhibition,
        London, England, 1992
The End of Architecture?, Austrian Museum of Applied Art, Conference,
        Vienna, 1992
Gallery of Functional Art, Santa Monica, California, 1992

Projects
Office Building, Ibiza, Spain
Billa Warenhandel AG Commercial Center, Vienna
Rhino Records Headquarters, Culver City, California
Samitaur Offices, Los Angeles
Very Large Array Sun Drawing Project, Socorro, New Mexico
P & D House, Los Angeles
Weston/Lawson House, Los Angeles
Paramount/Lindblade Offices, Culver City, California
8522 National Offices, Culver City, California

Publications
Eric Owen Moss: Buildings and Projects. Foreword by Philip Johnson. Introduction
        by Wolf D. Prix. New York: Rizzoli, 1991.
Progressive Architecture, January, 1992
International Interiors 3, Winter, 1991
L.A. Architect, December, 1991
L'Architecture d'Aujourd' hui, October, 1990
Architecture, June, 1990

Stanley Saitowitz Office

Stanley Saitowitz Born 1949; Johannesburg, South Africa

Education
University of Witwatersrand
University of California at Berkeley

Academic Affiliations
Professor, University of California at Berkeley
Elliot Noyes Professor, Harvard University Graduate School of Design

Exhibitions
Universe City, University Art Museum, Berkeley, California, 1985
G.A. Show, Tokyo, Japan, 1987
Poetic Constructs, Contemporary Realist Gallery, San Francisco, California, 1991
Transformed Structure, Security Pacific Gallery, San Francisco, California, 1991
Geological Architecture, Walker Art Center, Minneapolis; San Francisco
             Museum of Modern Art; Harvard University Graduate School of
             Design, 1991–92

Projects
New England Holocaust Memorial, Boston, Massachusetts, 1991
Mill Race Park Structures, Columbus, Indiana, 1990
Geological Architecture, Walker Art Center, Minneapolis, Minnesota, 1990
Byron Meyer Residence, Sonoma, California, 1989
1022 Natoma Street, Live/Work Building, San Francisco, California, 1989
American Memorial Library, Berlin, 1988
Di Napoli Residence, Los Gatos, California, 1987
McDonald Residence, Stinson Beach, California, 1987
1160 Bryant Street, Loft Renovation, San Francisco, California, 1986
California Museum of Photography, Riverside, California, 1986
Quady Winery, Madera, California, 1983

Publications
Architectural Review, February, 1988
Architectural Record, April, 1990
Progressive Architecture, September, 1990, November, 1990
G.A. Houses 28, 29, and *31,* Tokyo, 1990, 1991

Studio Works

Robert Mangurian   Born 1941; Baltimore, Maryland

Education
Stanford University, 1959–61
University of California at Berkeley, 1963–67

Awards
Progressive Architecture Awards and Citations, 1972, 1976, 1982, 1986, 1992
Rome Prize, NEA Mid-Career Fellowship, American Academy in Rome, 1977
National Endowment for the Arts Awards, 1978, 1980, 1988

Academic Affiliations
Director, Graduate Program, Southern California Institute of Architecture
Founder, principal researcher, Atelier Italia

Projects
South Side Settlement, Columbus, Ohio, 1974–80
Gilcrest House, Hollywood, California, 1983–85
Hadrian's Villa: A New Survey, 1985–present (with Mary-Ann Ray)
Grand Center Master Plan, St. Louis, Missouri, 1988–91 (with Mary-Ann Ray)
510 Brooks, Venice, California, 1988–present

Mary-Ann Ray   Born 1958; Seattle, Washington

Education
University of Washington, 1977–1981
Yale University, 1980
Southern California Institute of Architecture, 1985
Princeton University, 1987

Awards
Ford Foundation Grants in the Fine Arts, 1979, 1980, 1981
Progressive Architecture Awards, 1985, 1991
Rome Prize, American Academy in Rome, 1987–88
Graham Foundation Grant, 1990–91

Academic Affiliations
Faculty, Southern California Institute of Architecture
Co-Director, Atelier Italia

Projects
Re: American Dream—New Urban House Types for Los Angeles, 1990–1991
Perris Civic Center, Perris, California, 1991

Project Teams

Frank O. Gehry & Associates, Inc.

Principal/Designer
Frank O. Gehry

Principal/Manager
David Dentou

Team
Tom Buresh
Bruce Biesman-Simmons
Bruce Toman
C. Gregory Walsh

Photography
Frank O. Gehry & Associates
Wolfgang Hoyt Photography

Craig Hodgetts & Hsin-Ming Fung

Principals
Craig Hodgetts
Hsin-Ming Fung
Bob Bangham
Lynn Batsch
Frank Clementi
Chris Lawson
Maggie Ross
Peter Saal
Michael Swischuck

Photography
Neil Frankel

Holt Hinshaw Pfau Jones Architecture

'29 Chaise Longue Team
Wes Jones
Peter Pfau
Paul Holt
Marc Hinshaw
Richard Curl
Chris Palumbo
Ken Draizen
Robert Filler
Kai Klaasen

Either/Origins
Wes Jones

Photography
Neil Frankel
Mark Darley/Esto

Alcatraz Team
Wes Jones
Peter Pfau
Paul Holt
Marc Hinshaw
Dana Barber
Jane Chun
Tim Contreras
David Gadarian
Lourdes Garcia
Jeff Logan
Doug Mar
Minh Ngyen
Jim Park
Jean Young

Lifeguard Tower
Wes Jones
Peter Pfau
Paul Holt
Marc Hinshaw
David Gadarian
Lourdes Garcia
Doug Mar
Jim Park

Photography
Holt Hinshaw Pfau Jones

Franklin D. Israel Design Associates

Principal
Frank Israel

Hague House Architect
Annie Chu

Hague House Associate
Jay Deguchi

Baldwin House Architect
Steven Shortridge

Baldwin House Associate
Jay Deguchi

Models and Etchings Team
Annie Chu
Danny Kaplan

Design Consultant
Paul Fischer

Fabricators
Dyansen Studio
Karen Elmore
Paul Fischer
IMI Titanium, TiTech
Bijoy Jain
Princess Jewelry
Patrick Shaddau
Jim Tsai

Koning Eizenberg Architecture

Principals
Julie Eizenberg
Hendrik Koning

Developer and Associate Architect
Glenn Robert Erikson

Team
Tim Andreas
Stuart Emmons
Leem Jang Jong
Susan Stevens
David Woo

Photography
Brian Lane

Lubowicki Lanier

Principals
Susan Lanier
Paul Lubowicki

Team
Susan Addison
Benjamin Ball
Monika Furer
Randall Leffler
Brad Nettle
Bruce Resnick
Feliciano Reyes
David Spinelli
Matthew Tinner
Timothy Williams

Photography
Lubowicki Lanier

MACK Architects

Principal
Mark Mack

Team
Marianne Crivelli-Looser
Thomas Brandenberger

Photography
Mark Mack

Thom Mayne, Morphosis

Principal
Thom Mayne

Sixth Street House Project Architect
Kim Groves

Sixth Street House Team
Joey Shimoda
Maya Shimoguchi
Charlie Stout
Tim Swischuk
Andrew Zago

Barking Dog Team
Clark Stevens
Brendon McFarlane

Dancing Angel Team
Susan Lanier
Christopher Oakley

Photography
Tom Bonner
Farshid Assassi
Kim Zwarts

Eric Owen Moss Architect

Principal
Eric Owen Moss

Nara Convention Center Project Associate
Lucas Rios

Nara Team
Marco Benjamin
Su-shien Cho
Todd Conversano
Gevik Hovsepian
Sheng-yuan Hwang
Scott Nakao
José Pimentel
Elissa Scrafano
Ravindran Subramanian

Nara Photography
Tom Bonner
Todd Conversano

S.P.A.R.C I T Y Project Associate
Scott Nakao

S.P.A.R.C I T Y Team
Marco Benjamin
Todd Conversano
Mark Harris
Amanda Hyde
Lucas Rios
Ravindran Subramanian

S.P.A.R.C I T Y Photography
Todd Conversano

Stanley Saitowitz Office

Principal
Stanley Saitowitz

Project Architects
Daniel A. Luis
John Winder

Assistants
John Bass
Vincent Chew
David Lynch

Photography
Martin Zeitman

Studio Works

Principals
Robert Mangurian
Mary-Ann Ray

Team
Studio Works

Fabric
Victoria Shields

Photography
Robert Mangurian